WILLIAM SHAKESPEARE:
THE FIRST AND SECOND PARTS OF
KING HENRY IV

THE FIRST & SECOND PARTS OF

KING HENRY IV

By WILLIAM SHAKESPEARE

ILLUSTRATIONS BY JACK WOLFGANG BECK

PUBLISHED BY
GRAPHIC ARTS TYPOGRAPHERS, INC.
GEORGIAN LITHOGRAPHERS, INC.
FINCH, PRUYN & COMPANY, INC.
SENDOR BINDERY, INC.

INTRODUCTION — *A Kingly Father...A Princely Son*

King Henry IV, parts one and two, by William Shakespeare,
has been prepared as the fourth in a series of annual keepsakes
for the friends of the publishers.

Henry IV is probably Shakespeare's greatest historical play. The two parts
were completed in 1598 and are often performed together as they are quite
complementary. In fact, they may be viewed as the center of a trilogy beginning
with *Richard II* and ending with *Henry V.*

The touching relationship of Prince Harry (later King Henry V) to his father,
the King (previously Bolingbroke in *Richard II*), is woven into a historical
fabric along with the valiant Hotspur, the vapid Master Shallow and the
marvelously comic Sir John Falstaff. Sigmund Freud has assured us that
Sir John's humor arises "from the superiority of an ego which
neither his physical nor his moral defects can rob of its
cheerfulness and assurance."

The first Folio edition of 1623 was used as a guide in the preparation of this
book. The publishers are once again indebted to Jack Wolfgang Beck,
whose illustrations reflect sensitive attention to the details of the
play and whose time was generously given.

SCENE

Parts of England and Wales. Circa 1400.

DRAMATIS PERSONAE—Part I

KING HENRY IV, *King of England*

HENRY, *Prince of Wales, son to Henry IV*

PRINCE JOHN *of Lancaster, son to Henry IV*

EARL OF WESTMORELAND, *with the King's Party*

SIR WALTER BLUNT, *with the King's Party*

THOMAS PERCY, *Earl of Worcester*

HENRY PERCY, *Earl of Northumberland*

HENRY PERCY *("Hotspur"), his son*

EDMUND MORTIMER, *Earl of March*

RICHARD SCROOP, *Archbishop of York*

ARCHIBALD, *Earl of Douglas*

OWEN GLENDOWER, *opponent of the King*

SIR RICHARD VERNON, *opponent of the King*

SIR JOHN FALSTAFF, *irregular humorist*

SIR MICHAEL, *a friend of the Archbishop of York*

LADY PERCY, *Hotspur's wife and Mortimer's sister*

LADY MORTIMER, *Glendower's daughter and Mortimer's wife*

MISTRESS QUICKLY, *hostess of the tavern*

POINS, GADSHILL, *irregular humorists*

PETO, BARDOLPH, *irregular humorists*

FRANCIS, *a waiter*

SHERIFF, VINTNER, CHAMBERLAIN, OSTLER, OTHERS

PART I ACT ONE

*[Enter the King, Lord John of Lancaster, the Earl
of Westmoreland, Sir Walter Blunt, with others]*

King. So shaken as we are, so wan with care,
Find we a time for frighted peace to pant
And breathe short-winded accents of new broils
To be commenced in stronds afar remote.
No more the thirsty entrance of this soil
Shall daub her lips with her own children's blood,
No more shall trenching war channel her fields,
Nor bruise her flow'rets with the armed hoofs
Of hostile paces. Those opposed eyes
Which, like the meteors of a troubled heaven,
All of one nature, of one substance bred,
Did lately meet in the intestine shock
And furious close of civil butchery,
Shall now in mutual well-beseeming ranks
March all one way and be no more opposed
Against acquaintance, kindred, and allies.
The edge of war, like an ill-sheathed knife,
No more shall cut his master. Therefore, friends,
As far as to the sepulcher of Christ —
Whose soldier now, under whose blessed cross
We are impressed and engaged to fight —
Forthwith a power of English shall we levy,
Whose arms were molded in their mother's womb

To chase these pagans in those holy fields
Over whose acres walked those blessed feet
Which fourteen hundred years ago were nailed
For our advantage on the bitter cross.
But this our purpose now is twelvemonth old,
And bootless 'tis to tell you we will go.
Therefor we meet not now. Then let me hear
Of you, my gentle cousin Westmoreland,
What yesternight our council did decree
In forwarding this dear expedience.

Westmoreland. My liege, this haste was hot in question
And many limits of the charge set down
But yesternight; when all athwart there came
A post from Wales, loaden with heavy news,
Whose worst was that the noble Mortimer,
Leading the men of Herefordshire to fight
Against the irregular and wild Glendower,
Was by the rude hands of that Welshman taken,
A thousand of his people butchered;
Upon whose dead corpse there was such misuse,
Such beastly shameless transformation
By those Welshwomen done, as may not be
Without much shame retold or spoken of.

King. It seems then that the tidings of this broil
Brake off our business for the Holy Land.

Westmoreland. This, matched with other, did, my gracious lord;
For more uneven and unwelcome news
Came from the north, and thus it did import:

On Holy-rood Day the gallant Hotspur there,
Young Harry Percy, and brave Archibald,
That ever-valiant and approved Scot,
At Holmedon met, where they did spend
A sad and bloody hour;
As by discharge of their artillery
And shape of likelihood the news was told;
For he that brought them, in the very heat
And pride of their contention did take horse,
Uncertain of the issue any way.

King. Here is a dear, a true industrious friend,
Sir Walter Blunt, new lighted from his horse,
Stained with the variation of each soil
Betwixt that Holmedon and this seat of ours,
And he hath brought us smooth and welcome news.
The Earl of Douglas is discomfited;
Ten thousand bold Scots, two and twenty knights,
Balked in their own blood did Sir Walter see
On Holmedon's plains. Of prisoners, Hotspur took
Mordake, Earl of Fife and eldest son
To beaten Douglas, and the Earl of Athol,
Of Murray, Angus, and Menteith.
And is not this an honorable spoil?
A gallant prize? Ha, cousin, is it not?

Westmoreland. In faith it is. A conquest for a prince to boast of.

King. Yea, there thou mak'st me sad, and mak'st me sin
In envy that my Lord Northumberland
Should be the father to so blest a son:

A son who is the theme of honor's tongue,
Amongst a grove the very straightest plant;
Who is sweet fortune's minion and her pride;
Whilst I, by looking on the praise of him,
See riot and dishonor stain the brow
Of my young Harry. O that it could be proved
That some night-tripping fairy had exchanged
In cradle clothes our children where they lay,
And called mine Percy, his Plantagenet!
Then would I have his Harry, and he mine.
But let him from my thoughts. What think you, coz,
Of this young Percy's pride? The prisoners
Which he in this adventure hath surprised
To his own use he keeps, and sends me word
I shall have none but Mordake, Earl of Fife.

Westmoreland. This is his uncle's teaching, this is Worcester,
Malevolent to you in all aspects;
Which makes him prune himself and bristle up
The crest of youth against your dignity.

King. But I have sent for him to answer this;
And for this cause awhile we must neglect
Our holy purpose to Jerusalem.
Cousin, on Wednesday next our council we
Will hold at Windsor, so inform the lords:
But come yourself with speed to us again,
For more is to be said and to be done
Than out of anger can be uttered.

Westmoreland. I will, my liege. [*Exeunt*]

[Enter Prince of Wales and Sir John Falstaff]

Falstaff. Now, Hal, what time of day is it, lad?

Prince. Thou art so fat-witted with drinking of old sack, and unbuttoning thee after supper, and sleeping upon benches after noon, that thou hast forgotten to demand that truly which thou wouldest truly know. What a devil hast thou to do with the time of the day? Unless hours were cups of sack, and minutes capons, and clocks the tongues of bawds, and dials the signs of leaping houses, and the blessed sun himself a fair hot wench in flame-colored taffeta, I see no reason why thou shouldst be so superfluous to demand the time of the day.

Falstaff. Indeed you come near me now, Hal; for we that take purses go by the moon and the seven stars, and not by Phoebus, he, that wand'ring knight so fair. And I prithee, sweet wag, when thou art a king, as, God save thy Grace—Majesty I should say, for grace thou wilt have none—

Prince. What, none?

Falstaff. No, by my troth; not so much as will serve to be prologue to an egg and butter.

Prince. Well, how then? Come, roundly, roundly.

Falstaff. Marry, then, sweet wag, when thou art king, let not us that are squires of the night's body be called thieves of the day's beauty. Let us be Diana's foresters, gentlemen of the shade, minions of the moon; and let men say we be men of good government, being governed, as the sea is, by our noble and chaste mistress the moon, under whose countenance we steal.

Prince. Thou sayest well, and it holds well too; for the fortune of us that are the moon's men doth ebb and flow like the sea, being governed as the sea is by the moon. As, for proof now: a purse of gold most resolutely snatched on Monday night and most dissolutely spent on Tuesday morning; got with swearing "Lay by," and spent with crying "Bring in"; now in as low an ebb as the foot of the ladder, and by and by in as high a flow as the ridge of the gallows.

Falstaff. By the Lord, thou say'st true, lad—and is not my hostess of the tavern a most sweet wench?

Prince. As the honey of Hybla, my old lad of the castle—and is not a buff jerkin a most sweet robe of durance?

Falstaff. How now, how now, mad wag? What, in thy quips and thy quiddities? What a plague have I to do with a buff jerkin?

Prince. Why, what a pox have I to do with my hostess of the tavern?

Falstaff. Well, thou hast called her to a reckoning many a time and oft.

Prince. Did I ever call for thee to pay thy part?

Falstaff. No; I'll give thee thy due, thou hast paid all there.

Prince. Yea, and elsewhere, so far as my coin would stretch; and where it would not, I have used my credit.

Falstaff. Yea, and so used it that, were it not here apparent that thou art heir apparent— But I prithee, sweet wag, shall there be gallows standing in England when thou art king? And resolution thus fubbed as it is with the rusty curb of old father Antic the law? Do not thou, when thou art king, hang a thief.

Prince. No; thou shalt.

Falstaff. Shall I? O rare! By the Lord, I'll be a brave judge.

Prince. Thou judgest false already. I mean, thou shalt have the hanging of the thieves and so become a rare hangman.

Falstaff. Well, Hal, well; and in some sort it jumps with my humor as well as waiting in the court, I can tell you.

Prince. For obtaining of suits?

Falstaff. Yea, for obtaining of suits, whereof the hangman hath no lean wardrobe. 'Sblood, I am as melancholy as a gib-cat or a lugged bear.

Prince.	Or an old lion, or a lover's lute.
Falstaff.	Yea, or the drone of a Lincolnshire bagpipe.
Prince.	What sayest thou to a hare, or the melancholy of Moorditch?
Falstaff.	Thou hast the most unsavory similes, and art indeed the most comparative, rascalliest, sweet young prince. But, Hal, I prithee trouble me no more with vanity. I would to God thou and I knew where a commodity of good names were to be bought. An old lord of the council rated me the other day in the street about you, sir, but I marked him not; and yet he talked very wisely, but I regarded him not; and yet he talked wisely, and in the street too.
Prince.	Thou didst well, for wisdom cries out in the streets, and no man regards it.
Falstaff.	O, thou hast damnable iteration, and art indeed able to corrupt a saint. Thou hast done much harm upon me, Hal—God forgive thee for it! Before I knew thee, Hal, I knew nothing; and now am I, if a man should speak truly, little better than one of the wicked. I must give over this life, and I will give it over! By the Lord, and I do not, I am a villain! I'll be damned for never a king's son in Christendom.
Prince.	Where shall we take a purse tomorrow, Jack?
Falstaff.	Zounds, where thou wilt, lad! I'll make one. An I do not, call me villain and baffle me.
Prince.	I see a good amendment of life in thee—from praying to purse-taking.
Falstaff.	Why, Hal, 'tis my vocation, Hal. 'Tis no sin for a man to labor in his vocation.
	[*Enter Poins*]
	Poins! Now shall we know if Gadshill have set a match. O, if men were to be saved by merit, what hole in hell were hot enough for him? This is the most omnipotent villain that ever cried "Stand!" to a true man.
Prince.	Good morrow, Ned.
Poins.	Good morrow, sweet Hal. What says Monsieur Remorse? What says Sir John

Sack and Sugar? Jack, how agrees the devil and thee about thy soul, that thou soldest him on Good Friday last for a cup of Madeira and a cold capon's leg?

Prince. Sir John stands to his word, the devil shall have his bargain; for he was never yet a breaker of proverbs. He will give the devil his due.

Poins. Then art thou damned for keeping thy word with the devil.

Prince. Else he had been damned for cozening the devil.

Poins. But, my lads, my lads, tomorrow morning, by four o'clock early, at Gad's Hill! There are pilgrims going to Canterbury with rich offerings, and traders riding to London with fat purses. I have vizards for you all; you have horses for yourselves. Gadshill lies tonight in Rochester. I have bespoke supper tomorrow night in Eastcheap. We may do it as secure as sleep. If you will go, I will stuff your purses full of crowns; if you will not, tarry at home and be hanged!

Falstaff. Hear ye, Yedward: if I tarry at home and go not, I'll hang you for going.

Poins. You will, chops?

Falstaff. Hal, wilt thou make one?

Prince. Who, I rob? I a thief? Not I, by my faith.

Falstaff. There's neither honesty, manhood, nor good fellowship in thee, nor thou cam'st not of the blood royal if thou darest not stand for ten shillings.

Prince. Well then, once in my days I'll be a madcap.

Falstaff. Why, that's well said.

Prince. Well, come what will, I'll tarry at home.

Falstaff. By the Lord, I'll be a traitor then, when thou art king.

Prince. I care not.

Poins. Sir John, I prithee, leave the Prince and me alone. I will lay him down such reasons for this adventure that he shall go.

Falstaff. Well, God give thee the spirit of persuasion and him the ears of profiting, that what thou speakest may move and what he hears may be believed, that the true prince may (for recreation sake) prove a false thief; for the poor abuses of the time want countenance. Farewell; you shall find me in Eastcheap.

Prince. Farewell, the latter spring! Farewell, All-hallown summer! [*Exit Falstaff*]

Poins. Now, my good sweet honey lord, ride with us tomorrow. I have a jest to execute that I cannot manage alone. Falstaff, Bardolph, Peto, and Gadshill shall rob those men that we have already waylaid; yourself and I will not be there; and when they have the booty, if you and I do not rob them, cut this head off from my shoulders.

Prince. How shall we part with them in setting forth?

Poins. Why, we will set forth before or after them and appoint them a place of meeting, wherein it is at our pleasure to fail; and then will they adventure upon the exploit themselves, which they shall have no sooner achieved, but we'll set upon them.

Prince. Yea, but 'tis like that they will know us by our horses, by our habits, and by every other appointment, to be ourselves.

Poins. Tut! Our horses they shall not see—I'll tie them in the wood; our vizards we will change after we leave them; and, sirrah, I have cases of buckram for the nonce, to immask our noted outward garments.

Prince. Yea, but I doubt they will be too hard for us.

Poins. Well, for two of them, I know them to be as true-bred cowards as ever turned back; and for the third, if he fight longer than he sees reason, I'll forswear arms. The virtue of this jest will be the incomprehensible lies that this same fat rogue will tell us when we meet at supper: how thirty, at least, he fought with; what wards, what blows, what extremities he endured; and in the reproof of this lives the jest.

Prince. Well, I'll go with thee. Provide us all things necessary and meet me tomorrow night in Eastcheap. There I'll sup. Farewell.

Poins. Farewell, my lord. [*Exit*]

Prince. I know you all, and will awhile uphold
The unyoked humor of your idleness.
Yet herein will I imitate the sun,
Who doth permit the base contagious clouds
To smother up his beauty from the world,
That, when he please again to be himself,
Being wanted, he may be more wond'red at
By breaking through the foul and ugly mists
Of vapors that did seem to strangle him.
If all the year were playing holidays,
To sport would be as tedious as to work;
But when they seldom come, they wished-for come,
And nothing pleaseth but rare accidents.
So when this loose behavior I throw off
And pay the debt I never promised,
By how much better than my word I am,
By so much shall I falsify men's hopes;
And, like bright metal on a sullen ground,
My reformation, glitt'ring o'er my fault,
Shall show more goodly and attract more eyes
Than that which hath no foil to set it off.
I'll so offend to make offense a skill,
Redeeming time when men think least I will.
    [Exit]

[Enter the King, Northumberland, Worcester,
Hotspur, Sir Walter Blunt, with several others]

King. My blood hath been too cold and temperate,
Unapt to stir at these indignities,
And you have found me, for accordingly
You tread upon my patience; but be sure
I will from henceforth rather be myself,
Mighty and to be feared, than my condition,
Which hath been smooth as oil, soft as young down,
And therefore lost that title of respect
Which the proud soul ne'er pays but to the proud.

Worcester. Our house, my sovereign liege, little deserves
The scourge of greatness to be used on it—
And that same greatness too which our own hands
Have holp to make so portly.

Northumberland.   My lord—

King. Worcester, get thee gone, for I do see
Danger and disobedience in thine eye.
O, sir, your presence is too bold and peremptory,
And majesty might never yet endure
The moody frontier of a servant brow.
You have good leave to leave us: when we need
Your use and counsel, we shall send for you.

  [Exit Worcester]

You were about to speak.

Northumberland.   Yea, my good lord.
Those prisoners in your Highness' name demanded
Which Harry Percy here at Holmedon took,
Were, as he says, not with such strength denied
As is delivered to your Majesty.
Either envy, therefore, or misprision
Is guilty of this fault, and not my son.

Hotspur. My liege, I did deny no prisoners.
But I remember, when the fight was done,
When I was dry with rage and extreme toil,
Breathless and faint, leaning upon my sword,
Came there a certain lord, neat and trimly dressed,
Fresh as a bridegroom, and his chin new reaped
Showed like a stubble land at harvest home.
He was perfumed like a milliner,
And 'twixt his finger and his thumb he held
A pouncet box, which ever and anon
He gave his nose, and took't away again;
Who therewith angry, when it next came there,
Took it in snuff; and still he smiled and talked;
And as the soldiers bore dead bodies by,
He called them untaught knaves, unmannerly,
To bring a slovenly unhandsome corse
Betwixt the wind and his nobility.
With many holiday and lady terms
He questioned me, amongst the rest demanded
My prisoners in your Majesty's behalf.

I then, all smarting with my wounds being cold,
To be so pest'red with a popingay,
Out of my grief and my impatience
Answered neglectingly, I know not what—
He should, or he should not; for he made me mad
To see him shine so brisk, and smell so sweet,
And talk so like a waiting gentlewoman
Of guns and drums and wounds—God save the mark!—
And telling me the sovereignest thing on earth
Was parmacity for an inward bruise,
And that it was great pity, so it was,
This villainous saltpeter should be digged
Out of the bowels of the harmless earth,
Which many a good tall fellow had destroyed
So cowardly, and but for these vile guns,
He would himself have been a soldier.
This bald unjointed chat of his, my lord,
I answered indirectly, as I said,
And I beseech you, let not his report
Come current for an accusation
Betwixt my love and your high Majesty.

Blunt. The circumstance considered, good my lord,
Whate'er Harry Percy then had said
To such a person, and in such a place,
At such a time, with all the rest retold,
May reasonably die, and never rise
To do him wrong, or any way impeach
What then he said, so he unsay it now.

King. Why, yet he doth deny his prisoners,
But with proviso and exception,
That we at our own charge shall ransom straight
His brother-in-law, the foolish Mortimer;
Who, on my soul, hath willfully betrayed
The lives of those that he did lead to fight
Against that great magician, damned Glendower—
Whose daughter, as we hear, that Earl of March
Hath lately married. Shall our coffers, then,
Be emptied to redeem a traitor home?
Shall we buy treason, and indent with fears
When they have lost and forfeited themselves?
No, on the barren mountains let him starve!
For I shall never hold that man my friend
Whose tongue shall ask me for one penny cost
To ransom home revolted Mortimer.

Hotspur.   Revolted Mortimer?
He never did fall off, my sovereign liege,
But by the chance of war. To prove that true
Needs no more but one tongue for all those wounds,
Those mouthed wounds, which valiantly he took
When on the gentle Severn's sedgy bank,
In single opposition hand to hand,
He did confound the best part of an hour
In changing hardiment with great Glendower.
Three times they breathed; and three times did they drink,
Upon agreement, of swift Severn's flood;
Who then affrighted with their bloody looks
Ran fearfully among the trembling reeds
And hid his crisp head in the hollow bank,
Bloodstained with these valiant combatants.
Never did bare and rotten policy
Color her working with such deadly wounds;
Nor never could the noble Mortimer
Receive so many, and all willingly.
Then let not him be slandered with revolt.

King.	Thou dost belie him, Percy, thou dost belie him!
	He never did encounter with Glendower.
	I tell thee, he durst as well have met the devil alone
	As Owen Glendower for an enemy.
	Art thou not ashamed? But, sirrah, henceforth
	Let me not hear you speak of Mortimer.
	Send me your prisoners with the speediest means,
	Or you shall hear in such a kind from me
	As will displease you. My Lord Northumberland,
	We license your departure with your son.
	Send us your prisoners, or you will hear of it.

[Exit King, with Blunt, and train]

Hotspur.	And if the devil come and roar for them,
	I will not send them. I will after straight
	And tell him so, for I will ease my heart,
	Albeit I make a hazard of my head.
Northumberland.	What, drunk with choler? Stay, and pause awhile.
	Here comes your uncle.

[Enter Worcester]

Hotspur.	Speak of Mortimer?
	Zounds, I will speak of him, and let my soul
	Want mercy if I do not join with him!
	Yea, on his part I'll empty all these veins,
	And shed my dear blood drop by drop in the dust,
	But I will lift the downtrod Mortimer
	As high in the air as this unthankful king,
	As this ingrate and cank'red Bolingbroke.

Northumberland.	Brother, the King hath made your nephew mad.
Worcester.	Who struck this heat up after I was gone?
Hotspur.	He will forsooth have all my prisoners;
	And when I urged the ransom once again
	Of my wife's brother, then his cheek looked pale,
	And on my face he turned an eye of death,
	Trembling even at the name of Mortimer.
Worcester.	I cannot blame him. Was not he proclaimed
	By Richard that dead is, the next of blood?
Northumberland.	He was, I heard the proclamation:
	And then it was when the unhappy king
	(Whose wrongs in us God pardon!) did set forth
	Upon his Irish expedition;
	From whence he intercepted did return
	To be deposed, and shortly murdered.
Worcester.	And for whose death we in the world's wide mouth
	Live scandalized and foully spoken of.
Hotspur.	But soft, I pray you, did King Richard then
	Proclaim my brother Edmund Mortimer
	Heir to the crown?
Northumberland.	He did, myself did hear it.

Hotspur.   Nay, then I cannot blame his cousin king,
That wished him on the barren mountains starve.
But shall it be that you, that set the crown
Upon the head of this forgetful man,
And for his sake wear the detested blot
Of murderous subornation—shall it be
That you a world of curses undergo,
Being the agents or base second means,
The cords, the ladder, or the hangman rather?
O, pardon me that I descend so low
To show the line and the predicament
Wherein you range under this subtle king!
Shall it for shame be spoken in these days,
Or fill up chronicles in time to come,
That men of your nobility and power
Did gage them both in an unjust behalf
(As both of you, God pardon it, have done)
To put down Richard, that sweet lovely rose,
And plant this thorn, this canker Bolingbroke?
And shall it in more shame be further spoken
That you are fooled, discarded, and shook off
By him for whom these shames ye underwent?
No, yet time serves wherein you may redeem
Your banished honors and restore yourselves
Into the good thoughts of the world again;
Revenge the jeering and disdained contempt
Of this proud king, who studies day and night

To answer all the debt he owes to you
Even with the bloody payment of your deaths.
Therefore I say —

Worcester.   Peace, cousin, say no more;
And now I will unclasp a secret book,
And to your quick-conceiving discontents
I'll read you matter deep and dangerous,
As full of peril and adventurous spirit
As to o'erwalk a current roaring loud
On the unsteadfast footing of a spear.

Hotspur.   If he fall in, good night, or sink, or swim!
Send danger from the east unto the west,
So honor cross it from the north to south,
And let them grapple. O, the blood more stirs
To rouse a lion than to start a hare!

Northumberland.   Imagination of some great exploit
Drives him beyond the bounds of patience.

Hotspur.   By heaven, methinks it were an easy leap
To pluck bright honor from the pale-faced moon,
Or dive into the bottom of the deep,
Where fathom line could never touch the ground,
And pluck up drowned honor by the locks,
So he that doth redeem her thence might wear
Without corrival all her dignities;
But out upon this half-faced fellowship!

Worcester.	He apprehends a world of figures here,
	But not the form of what he should attend.
	Good cousin, give me audience for a while.
Hotspur.	I cry you mercy.
Worcester.	Those same noble Scots that are your prisoners—
Hotspur.	I'll keep them all.
	By God, he shall not have a Scot of them!
	No, if a Scot would save his soul, he shall not.
	I'll keep them, by this hand!
Worcester.	You start away
	And lend no ear unto my purposes.
	Those prisoners you shall keep.
Hotspur.	Nay, I will! That's flat!
	He said he would not ransom Mortimer,
	Forbade my tongue to speak of Mortimer,
	But I will find him when he lies asleep,
	And in his ear I'll hollo "Mortimer."
	Nay, I'll have a starling shall be taught to speak
	Nothing but "Mortimer," and give it him
	To keep his anger still in motion.
Worcester.	Hear you, cousin, a word.
Hotspur.	All studies here I solemnly defy
	Save how to gall and pinch this Bolingbroke;
	And that same sword-and-buckler Prince of Wales,
	But that I think his father loves him not
	And would be glad he met with some mischance,
	I would have him poisoned with a pot of ale.

Worcester.	Farewell, kinsman: I'll talk to you
	When you are better tempered to attend.
Northumberland.	Why, what a wasp-stung and impatient fool
	Art thou to break into this woman's mood,
	Tying thine ear to no tongue but thine own!
Hotspur.	Why, look you, I am whipped and scourged with rods,
	Nettled, and stung with pismires, when I hear
	Of this vile politician, Bolingbroke.
	In Richard's time—what do you call the place?
	A plague upon it! It is in Gloucestershire;
	'Twas where the madcap duke his uncle kept,
	His uncle York—where I first bowed my knee
	Unto this king of smiles, this Bolingbroke—
	'Sblood!—when you and he came back from Ravenspurgh—
Northumberland.	At Berkeley Castle.
Hotspur.	You say true.
	Why, what a candy deal of courtesy
	This fawning greyhound then did proffer me!
	"Look when his infant fortune came to age,"
	And "gentle Harry Percy," and "kind cousin"—
	O, the devil take such cozeners!—God forgive me!
	Good uncle, tell your tale; I have done.

Worcester.	Nay, if you have not, to it again.
	We will stay your leisure.
Hotspur.	I have done, i' faith.
Worcester.	Then once more to your Scottish prisoners:
	Deliver them up without their ransom straight,
	And make the Douglas' son your only mean
	For powers in Scotland—which, for divers reasons
	Which I shall send you written, be assured
	Will easily be granted. [*To Northumberland*] You, my lord,
	Your son in Scotland being thus employed,
	Shall secretly into the bosom creep
	Of that same noble prelate well-beloved,
	The Archbishop.
Hotspur.	Of York, is it not?
Worcester.	True; who bears hard
	His brother's death at Bristow, the Lord Scroop.
	I speak not this in estimation,
	As what I think might be, but what I know
	Is ruminated, plotted, and set down,
	And only stays but to behold the face
	Of that occasion that shall bring it on.
Hotspur.	I smell it. Upon my life, it will do well.
Northumberland.	Before the game is afoot thou still let'st slip.
Hotspur.	Why, it cannot choose but be a noble plot.
	And then the power of Scotland and of York
	To join with Mortimer, ha?
Worcester.	And so they shall.

Hotspur.	In faith, it is exceedingly well aimed.
Worcester.	And 'tis no little reason bids us speed
	To save our heads by raising of a head;
	For, bear ourselves as even as we can,
	The King will always think him in our debt,
	And think we think ourselves unsatisfied,
	Till he hath found a time to pay us home.
	And see already how he doth begin
	To make us strangers to his looks of love.
Hotspur.	He does, he does! We'll be revenged on him.
Worcester.	Cousin, farewell. No further go in this
	Than I by letters shall direct your course.
	When time is ripe, which will be suddenly,
	I'll steal to Glendower and Lord Mortimer,
	Where you and Douglas, and our pow'rs at once,
	As I will fashion it, shall happily meet,
	To bear our fortunes in our own strong arms,
	Which now we hold at much uncertainty.
Northumberland.	Farewell, good brother. We shall thrive, I trust.
Hotspur.	Uncle, adieu. O, let the hours be short
	Till fields and blows and groans applaud our sport!
	[Exeunt]

PART I ACT TWO

ROCHESTER: AN INN YARD

[Enter a Carrier with a lantern in his hand]

First Carrier.   Heigh-ho! An it be not four by the day, I'll be hanged. Charles' wain is over the new chimney, and yet our horse not packed. What, ostler!

Ostler.   *[Within]* Anon, anon.

First Carrier.   I prithee, Tom, beat Cut's saddle, put a few flocks in the point; poor jade is wrung in the withers out of all cess.

[Enter another Carrier]

Second Carrier.   Peas and beans are as dank here as a dog, and that is the next way to give poor jades the bots. This house is turned upside down since Robin Ostler died.

First Carrier.   Poor fellow never joyed since the price of oats rose; it was the death of him.

Second Carrier.   I think this be the most villainous house in all London road for fleas, I am stung like a tench.

First Carrier.   Like a tench? By the mass, there is ne'er a king christen could be better bit than I have been since the first cock.

Second Carrier.   Why, they will allow us ne'er a jordan, and then we leak in your chimney, and your chamber-lye breeds fleas like a loach.

First Carrier.   What, ostler! Come away and be hanged! Come away!

Second Carrier.   I have a gammon of bacon and two razes of ginger, to be delivered as far as Charing Cross.

First Carrier.   God's body! The turkeys in my pannier are quite starved. What, ostler! A plague on thee, hast thou never an eye in thy head? Canst not hear? And 'twere not as good deed as drink to break the pate on thee, I am a very villain. Come, and be hanged! Hast no faith in thee?

[Enter Gadshill]

Gadshill.   Good morrow, carriers, what's o'clock?

First Carrier.	I think it be two o'clock.
Gadshill.	I prithee lend me thy lantern to see my gelding in the stable.
First Carrier.	Nay, by God, soft! I know a trick worth two of that, i' faith.
Gadshill.	I pray thee lend me thine.
Second Carrier.	Ay, when? Canst tell? Lend me thy lantern, quoth he? Marry, I'll see thee hanged first!
Gadshill.	Sirrah carrier, what time do you mean to come to London?
Second Carrier.	Time enough to go to bed with a candle, I warrant thee. Come, neighbor Mugs, we'll call up the gentlemen, they will along with company, for they have great charge.
	{*Exeunt Carriers*}
Gadshill.	What, ho! Chamberlain!
	{*Enter Chamberlain*}
Chamberlain.	"At hand, quoth pickpurse."
Gadshill.	That's even as fair as "at hand, quoth the chamberlain"; for thou variest no more from picking of purses than giving direction doth from laboring: thou layest the plot how.
Chamberlain.	Good morrow, Master Gadshill. It holds current that I told you yesternight: there's a franklin in the Wild of Kent hath brought three hundred marks with him in gold, I heard him tell it to one of his company last night at supper—a kind of auditor, one that hath abundance of charge too, God knows what. They are up already and call for eggs and butter, they will away presently.
Gadshill.	Sirrah, if they meet not with Saint Nicholas' clerks, I'll give thee this neck.
Chamberlain.	No, I'll none of it; I pray thee keep that for the hangman; for I know thou worshippest Saint Nicholas as truly as a man of falsehood may.
Gadshill.	What talkest thou to me of the hangman? If I hang, I'll make a fat pair of gallows; for if I hang, old Sir John hangs with me, and thou knowest he is no starveling. Tut! There are other Troyans that thou dream'st not of, the which for sport sake are content to do the profession some grace; that would (if matters should be looked into) for their own credit sake make all whole. I am joined with no foot-

landrakers, no long-staff sixpenny strikers, none of these mad mustachio purple-hued maltworms; but with nobility and tranquillity, burgomasters and great oneyers, such as can hold in, such as will strike sooner than speak, and speak sooner than drink, and drink sooner than pray—and yet, zounds, I lie, for they pray continually to their saint, the commonwealth, or rather, not pray to her, but prey on her, for they ride up and down on her and make her their boots.

Chamberlain. What, the commonwealth their boots? Will she hold out water in foul way?

Gadshill. She will, she will! Justice hath liquored her. We steal as in a castle, cocksure. We have the receipt of fernseed, we walk invisible.

Chamberlain. Nay, by my faith, I think you are more beholding to the night than to fernseed for your walking invisible.

Gadshill. Give me thy hand. Thou shalt have a share in our purchase, as I am a true man.

Chamberlain. Nay, rather let me have it, as you are a false thief.

Gadshill. Go to; "homo" is a common name to all men. Bid the ostler bring my gelding out of the stable. Farewell, you muddy knave.

[*Exeunt*]

[Enter Prince, Poins, and Peto, etc.]

Poins. Come, shelter, shelter! I have removed Falstaff's horse, and he frets like a gummed velvet.

Prince. Stand close. *[They step aside]*

[Enter Falstaff]

Falstaff. Poins! Poins, and be hanged! Poins!

Prince. *[Comes forward]* Peace, ye fat-kidneyed rascal! What a brawling dost thou keep!

Falstaff. Where's Poins, Hal?

Prince. He is walked up to the top of the hill; I'll go seek him. *[Steps aside]*

Falstaff. I am accursed to rob in that thief's company. The rascal hath removed my horse and tied him I know not where. If I travel but four foot by the squire further afoot, I shall break my wind. Well, I doubt not but to die a fair death for all this, if I scape hanging for killing that rogue. I have forsworn his company hourly any time this two and twenty years, and yet I am bewitched with the rogue's company. If the rascal have not given me medicines to make me love him, I'll be hanged. It could not be else: I have drunk medicines. Poins! Hal! A plague upon you both! Bardolph! Peto! I'll starve ere I'll rob a foot further. And 'twere not as good a deed as drink to turn true man and to leave these rogues, I am the veriest varlet that ever chewed with a tooth. Eight yards of uneven ground is threescore and ten miles afoot with me, and the stony-hearted villains know it well enough. A plague upon it when thieves cannot be true one to another! *[They whistle]* Whew! A plague upon you all! Give me my horse, you rogues! Give me my horse and be hanged!

Prince. *[Comes forward]* Peace, ye fat-guts! Lie down, lay thine ear close to the ground, and list if thou canst hear the tread of travelers.

Falstaff.	Have you any levers to lift me up again, being down? 'Sblood, I'll not bear mine own flesh so far afoot again for all the coin in thy father's exchequer. What a plague mean ye to colt me thus?
Prince.	Thou liest, thou art not colted, thou art uncolted.
Falstaff.	I prithee, good Prince Hal, help me to my horse, good king's son.
Prince.	Out, ye rogue! Shall I be your ostler?
Falstaff.	Hang thyself in thine own heir-apparent garters! If I be ta'en, I'll peach for this. And I have not ballads made on you all, and sung to filthy tunes, let a cup of sack be my poison. When a jest is so forward—and afoot too—I hate it.
	[*Enter Gadshill and Bardolph*]
Gadshill.	Stand!
Falstaff.	So I do, against my will.
Poins.	O, 'tis our setter; I know his voice. [*Comes forward*] Bardolph, what news?
Bardolph.	Case ye, case ye! On with your vizards! There's money of the King's coming down the hill; 'tis going to the King's exchequer.
Falstaff.	You lie, ye rogue! 'Tis going to the King's tavern.
Gadshill.	There's enough to make us all—
Falstaff.	To be hanged.
Prince.	Sirs, you four shall front them in the narrow lane; Ned Poins and I will walk lower: if they scape from your encounter, then they light on us.

Peto.	How many be there of them?
Gadshill.	Some eight or ten.
Falstaff.	Zounds, will they not rob us?
Prince.	What, a coward, Sir John Paunch?
Falstaff.	Indeed, I am not John of Gaunt your grandfather, but yet no coward, Hal.
Prince.	Well, we leave that to the proof.
Poins.	Sirrah Jack, thy horse stands behind the hedge. When thou need'st him, there thou shalt find him. Farewell and stand fast.
Falstaff.	Now cannot I strike him, if I should be hanged.
Prince.	[*Aside to Poins*] Ned, where are our disguises?
Poins.	[*Aside to Prince*] Here, hard by. Stand close.
	[*Exeunt Prince and Poins*]
Falstaff.	Now, my masters, happy man be his dole, say I. Every man to his business.
	[*Enter the Travelers*]
Traveler.	Come, neighbor. The boy shall lead our horses down the hill; we'll walk afoot awhile and ease our legs.
Thieves.	Stand!
Traveler.	Jesus bless us!
Falstaff.	Strike! Down with them! Cut the villains' throats! Ah, whoreson caterpillars! Bacon-fed knaves! They hate us youth. Down with them! Fleece them!
Traveler.	O, we are undone, both we and ours forever!
Falstaff.	Hang ye, gorbellied knaves, are ye undone? No, ye fat chuffs; I would your store were here! On, bacons, on! What, ye knaves, young men must live. You are grandjurors, are ye? We'll jure ye, faith!
	[*Here they rob them and bind them. Exeunt*]

[Enter the Prince and Poins]

Prince. The thieves have bound the true men. Now could thou and I rob the thieves and go merrily to London, it would be argument for a week, laughter for a month, and a good jest forever.

Poins. Stand close! I hear them coming.

[They stand aside, and the thieves enter again]

Falstaff. Come, my masters, let us share, and then to horse before day. And the Prince and Poins be not two arrant cowards, there's no equity stirring. There's no more valor in that Poins than in a wild duck.

Prince. Your money!

[As they are sharing, the Prince and Poins set upon them. They all run away, and Falstaff, after a blow or two, runs away too, leaving the booty behind them]

Poins. Villains!

Prince. Got with much ease. Now merrily to horse. The thieves are all scattered, and possessed with fear so strongly that they dare not meet each other: each takes his fellow for an officer. Away, good Ned. Falstaff sweats to death and lards the lean earth as he walks along. Were't not for laughing, I should pity him.

Poins. How the fat rogue roared!

[Exeunt]

[Enter Hotspur solus, reading a letter]

Hotspur. "But, for mine own part, my lord, I could be well contented to be there, in respect of the love I bear your house." He could be contented—why is he not then? In respect of the love he bears our house! He shows in this he loves his own barn better than he loves our house. Let me see some more. "The purpose you undertake is dangerous"—why, that's certain! 'Tis dangerous to take a cold, to sleep, to drink; but I tell you, my lord fool, out of this nettle, danger, we pluck this flower, safety. "The purpose you undertake is dangerous, the friends you have named uncertain, the time itself unsorted, and your whole plot too light for the counterpoise of so great an opposition." Say you so, say you so? I say unto you again, you are a shallow, cowardly hind, and you lie. What a lack-brain is this! By the Lord, our plot is a good plot as ever was laid; our friends true and constant: a good plot, good friends, and full of expectation; an excellent plot, very good friends. What a frosty-spirited rogue is this! Why, my Lord of York commends the plot and the general course of the action. Zounds, and I were now by this rascal, I could brain him with his lady's fan. Is there not my father, my uncle, and myself; Lord Edmund Mortimer, my Lord of York, and Owen Glendower? Is there not, besides, the Douglas? Have I not all their letters to meet me in arms by the ninth of the next month, and are they not some of them set forward already? What a pagan rascal is this, an infidel! Ha! you shall see now, in very sincerity of fear and cold heart will he to the King and lay open all our proceedings. O, I could divide myself and go to buffets for moving such a dish of skim milk with so honorable an action! Hang him, let him tell the King! We are prepared. I will set forward tonight. *[Enter his Lady]*

How now, Kate? I must leave you within these two hours.

Lady. O my good lord, why are you thus alone?
For what offense have I this fortnight been
A banished woman from my Harry's bed?
Tell me, sweet lord, what is't that takes from thee
Thy stomach, pleasure, and thy golden sleep?
Why dost thou bend thine eyes upon the earth,
And start so often when thou sit'st alone?
Why hast thou lost the fresh blood in thy cheeks
And given my treasures and my rights of thee
To thick-eyed musing and cursed melancholy?
In thy faint slumbers I by thee have watched,
And heard thee murmur tales of iron wars,
Speak terms of manage to thy bounding steed,
Cry "Courage! To the field!" And thou hast talked
Of sallies and retires, of trenches, tents,
Of palisadoes, frontiers, parapets,
Of basilisks, of cannon, culverin,
Of prisoners' ransom, and of soldiers slain,
And all the currents of a heady fight.
Thy spirit within thee hath been so at war,
And thus hath so bestirred thee in thy sleep,
That beads of sweat have stood upon thy brow
Like bubbles in a late-disturbed stream,
And in thy face strange motions have appeared,
Such as we see when men restrain their breath
On some great sudden hest. O, what portents are these?
Some heavy business hath my lord in hand,
And I must know it, else he loves me not.

Hotspur.	What, ho!
	[Enter a Servant]
	Is Gilliams with the packet gone?
Servant.	He is, my lord, an hour ago.
Hotspur.	Hath Butler brought those horses from the sheriff?
Servant.	One horse, my lord, he brought even now.
Hotspur.	What horse? A roan, a crop-ear, is it not?
Servant.	It is, my lord.
Hotspur.	That roan shall be my throne. Well, I will back him straight. O Esperance! Bid Butler lead him forth into the park.
	[Exit Servant]
Lady.	But hear you, my lord.
Hotspur.	What say'st thou, my lady?
Lady.	What is it carries you away?
Hotspur.	Why, my horse, my love — my horse!
Lady.	Out, you mad-headed ape! A weasel hath not such a deal of spleen as you are tossed with. In faith, I'll know your business, Harry, that I will! I fear my brother Mortimer doth stir about his title and hath sent for you to line his enterprise; but if you go—
Hotspur.	So far afoot, I shall be weary, love.
Lady.	Come, come, you paraquito, answer me directly unto this question that I ask. In faith, I'll break thy little finger, Harry, and if thou wilt not tell me all things true.
Hotspur.	Away, away, you trifler! Love? I love thee not; I care not for thee, Kate. This is no world To play with mammets and to tilt with lips. We must have bloody noses and cracked crowns, And pass them current too. Gods me, my horse! What say'st thou, Kate? What wouldst thou have with me?

Lady.	Do you not love me? Do you not indeed?
	Well, do not then; for since you love me not,
	I will not love myself. Do you not love me?
	Nay, tell me if you speak in jest or no.
Hotspur.	Come, wilt thou see me ride?
	And when I am a-horseback, I will swear
	I love thee infinitely. But hark you, Kate:
	I must not have you henceforth question me
	Whither I go, nor reason whereabout.
	Whither I must, I must, and—to conclude,
	This evening must I leave you, gentle Kate.
	I know you wise—but yet no farther wise
	Than Harry Percy's wife; constant you are—
	But yet a woman; and for secrecy,
	No lady closer—for I well believe
	Thou wilt not utter what thou dost not know,
	And so far will I trust thee, gentle Kate—
Lady.	How? So far?
Hotspur.	Not an inch further. But hark you, Kate:
	Whither I go, thither shall you go too;
	Today will I set forth, tomorrow you.
	Wilt this content you, Kate?
Lady.	It must of force.

[Exeunt]

[Enter Prince and Poins]

Prince. Ned, prithee come out of that fat room and lend me thy hand to laugh a little.

Poins. Where hast been, Hal?

Prince. With three or four loggerheads amongst three or fourscore hogsheads. I have sounded the very bass-string of humility. Sirrah, I am sworn brother to a leash of drawers and can call them all by their christen names, as Tom, Dick, and Francis. They take it already upon their salvation that, though I be but Prince of Wales, yet I am the king of courtesy, and tell me flatly I am no proud Jack like Falstaff, but a Corinthian, a lad of mettle, a good boy (by the Lord, so they call me!), and when I am King of England I shall command all the good lads in Eastcheap. They call drinking deep, dyeing scarlet; and when you breathe in your watering, they cry "hem!" and bid you play it off. To conclude, I am so good a proficient in one quarter of an hour that I can drink with any tinker in his own language during my life. I tell thee, Ned, thou hast lost much honor that thou wert not with me in this action. But, sweet Ned—to sweeten which name of Ned, I give thee this pennyworth of sugar, clapped even now into my hand by an under-skinker, one that never spake other English in his life than "Eight shillings and sixpence," and "You are welcome," with this shrill addition, "Anon, anon, sir! Score a pint of bastard in the Half-moon," or so—but, Ned, to drive away the time till Falstaff come, I prithee do thou stand in some by-room while I question my puny drawer to what end he gave me the sugar; and do thou never leave calling "Francis!" that his tale to me may be nothing but "Anon!" Step aside, and I'll show thee a precedent.

Poins. Francis!

Prince.	Thou art perfect.
Poins.	Francis!

[Poins steps aside. Enter Francis, a Drawer]

Francis.	Anon, anon, sir. Look down into the Pomgarnet, Ralph.
Prince.	Come hither, Francis.
Francis.	My lord?
Prince.	How long has thou to serve, Francis?
Francis.	Forsooth, five years, and as much as to—
Poins.	*[Within]* Francis!
Francis.	Anon, anon, sir.
Prince.	Five year! By'r Lady, a long lease for the clinking of pewter. But, Francis, darest thou be so valiant as to play the coward with thy indenture and show it a fair pair of heels and run from it?
Francis.	O Lord, sir, I'll be sworn upon all the books in England I could find in my heart—
Poins.	*[Within]* Francis!
Francis.	Anon, sir.
Prince.	How old art thou, Francis?
Francis.	Let me see: about Michaelmas next I shall be—
Poins.	*[Within]* Francis!
Francis.	Anon, sir. Pray stay a little, my lord.
Prince.	Nay, but hark you, Francis. For the sugar thou gavest me—'twas a pennyworth, was't not?
Francis.	O Lord! I would it had been two!
Prince.	I will give thee for it a thousand pound. Ask me when thou wilt, and thou shalt have it.
Poins.	*[Within]* Francis!
Francis.	Anon, anon.
Prince.	Anon, Francis? No, Francis; but tomorrow, Francis; or, Francis, a Thursday; or indeed, Francis, when thou wilt. But, Francis—

Francis.	My lord?
Prince.	Wilt thou rob this leathern-jerkin, crystal-button, not-pated, agate-ring, puke-stocking, caddis-garter, smooth-tongue, Spanish-pouch?
Francis.	O Lord, sir, who do you mean?
Prince.	Why then, your brown bastard is your only drink; for look you, Francis, your white canvas doublet will sully. In Barbary, sir, it cannot come to so much.
Francis.	What, sir?
Poins.	[*Within*] Francis!
Prince.	Away, you rogue! Dost thou not hear them call?

[*They both call him. The Drawer stands amazed,
not knowing where to go. The Vintner enters*]

Vintner.	What, stand'st thou still, and hear'st such a calling? Look to the guests within.

[*Exit Francis*]

My lord, old Sir John, with half a dozen more, are at the door. Shall I let them in?

Prince.	Let them alone awhile, and then open the door.

[*Exit Vintner*]

Poins!

Poins.	[*Within*] Anon, anon, sir.

[*Enter Poins*]

Prince.	Sirrah, Falstaff and the rest of the thieves are at the door. Shall we be merry?
Poins.	As merry as crickets, my lad. But hark ye; what cunning match have you made with this jest of the drawer? Come, what's the issue?
Prince.	I am now of all humors that have showed themselves humors since the old days of goodman Adam to the pupil age of this present twelve o'clock at midnight.

[*Enter Francis*]

What's o'clock, Francis?

Francis.	Anon, anon, sir. [*Exit*]

Prince. That ever this fellow should have fewer words than a parrot, and yet the son of a woman! His industry is upstairs and downstairs, his eloquence the parcel of a reckoning. I am not yet of Percy's mind, the Hotspur of the North: he that kills me some six or seven dozen of Scots at a breakfast, washes his hands, and says to his wife, "Fie upon this quiet life! I want work." "O my sweet Harry," says she, "how many hast thou killed today?" "Give my roan horse a drench," says he, and answers "Some fourteen," an hour after, "a trifle, a trifle." I prithee call in Falstaff. I'll play Percy, and that damned brawn shall play Dame Mortimer his wife. "Rivo!" says the drunkard. Call in Ribs, call in Tallow.

> [*Enter Falstaff, Gadshill, Bardolph,
> and Peto; Francis follows with wine*]

Poins. Welcome, Jack. Where hast thou been?

Falstaff. A plague of all cowards, I say, and a vengeance too! Marry and amen! Give me a cup of sack, boy. Ere I lead this life long, I'll sew netherstocks, and mend them and foot them too. A plague of all cowards! Give me a cup of sack, rogue. Is there no virtue extant?

> [*He drinks*]

Prince. Didst thou never see Titan kiss a dish of butter (pitiful-hearted Titan!) that melted at the sweet tale of the sun's? If thou didst, then behold that compound.

Falstaff. You rogue, here's lime in this sack too! There is nothing but roguery to be found in villainous man. Yet a coward is worse than a cup of sack with lime in it—a villainous coward! Go thy ways, old Jack, die when thou wilt; if manhood, good manhood, be not forgot upon the face of the earth, then am I a shotten herring. There lives not three good men unhanged in England; and one of them is fat, and grows old. God help the while! A bad world, I say. I would I were a weaver; I could sing psalms or anything. A plague of all cowards, I say still!

Prince. How now, woolsack? What mutter you?

Falstaff.	A king's son! If I do not beat thee out of thy kingdom with a dagger of lath and drive all thy subjects afore thee like a flock of wild geese, I'll never wear hair on my face more. You Prince of Wales?
Prince.	Why, you whoreson round man, what's the matter?
Falstaff.	Are not you a coward? Answer me to that—and Poins there?
Poins.	Zounds, ye fat paunch, and ye call me coward, by the Lord, I'll stab thee.
Falstaff.	I call thee coward? I'll see thee damned ere I call thee coward, but I would give a thousand pound I could run as fast as thou canst. You are straight enough in the shoulders; you care not who sees your back. Call you that backing of your friends? A plague upon such backing, give me them that will face me. Give me a cup of sack. I am a rogue if I drunk today.
Prince.	O villain, thy lips are scarce wiped since thou drunk'st last.
Falstaff.	All is one for that. [*He drinks*] A plague of all cowards, still say I.
Prince.	What's the matter?
Falstaff.	What's the matter? There be four of us here have ta'en a thousand pound this day morning.
Prince.	Where is it, Jack, where is it?
Falstaff.	Where is it? Taken from us it is. A hundred upon poor four of us!
Prince.	What, a hundred, man?
Falstaff.	I am a rogue if I were not at half-sword with a dozen of them two hours together. I have scaped by miracle. I am eight times thrust through the doublet, four through the hose; my buckler cut through and through; my sword hacked like a handsaw—*ecce signum!* I never dealt better since I was a man. All would not do. A plague of all cowards! Let them speak. If they speak more or less than truth, they are villains and the sons of darkness.
Prince.	Speak, sirs. How was it?
Gadshill.	We four set upon some dozen—

Falstaff.	Sixteen at least, my lord.
Gadshill.	And bound them.
Peto.	No, no, they were not bound.
Falstaff.	You rogue, they were bound, every man of them, or I am a Jew else—an Ebrew Jew.
Gadshill.	As we were sharing, some six or seven fresh men set upon us—
Falstaff.	And unbound the rest, and then come in the other.
Prince.	What, fought you with them all?
Falstaff.	All? I know not what you call all, but if I fought not with fifty of them, I am a bunch of radish! If there were not two or three and fifty upon poor old Jack, then am I no two-legged creature.
Prince.	Pray God you have not murd'red some of them.
Falstaff.	Nay, that's past praying for. I have peppered two of them. Two I am sure I have paid, two rogues in buckram suits. I tell thee what, Hal—if I tell thee a lie, spit in my face, call me horse. Thou knowest my old ward: here I lay, and thus I bore my point. Four rogues in buckram let drive at me.
Prince.	What, four? Thou saidst but two even now.
Falstaff.	Four, Hal. I told thee four.
Poins.	Ay, ay, he said four.
Falstaff.	These four came all afront and mainly thrust at me. I made me no more ado but took all their seven points in my target, thus.
Prince.	Seven? Why, there were but four even now.
Falstaff.	In buckram?
Poins.	Ay, four, in buckram suits.
Falstaff.	Seven, by these hilts, or I am a villain else.
Prince.	[*Aside to Poins*] Prithee let him alone. We shall have more anon.
Falstaff.	Dost thou hear me, Hal?
Prince.	Ay, and mark thee too, Jack.

Falstaff. Do so, for it is worth the list'ning to. These nine in buckram that I told thee of—

Prince. So, two more already.

Falstaff. Their points being broken—

Poins. Down fell their hose.

Falstaff. Began to give me ground; but I followed me close, came in, foot and hand, and with a thought seven of the eleven I paid.

Prince. O monstrous! Eleven buckram men grown out of two!

Falstaff. But, as the devil would have it, three misbegotten knaves in Kendal green came at my back and let drive at me; for it was so dark, Hal, that thou couldest not see thy hand.

Prince. These lies are like their father that begets them—gross as a mountain, open, palpable. Why, thou clay-brained guts, thou knotty-pated fool, thou whoreson obscene greasy tallow-catch—

Falstaff. What, art thou mad? Art thou mad? Is not the truth the truth?

Prince. Why, how couldst thou know these men in Kendal green when it was so dark thou couldst not see thy hand? Come, tell us your reason. What sayest thou to this?

Poins. Come, your reason, Jack, your reason.

Falstaff. What, upon compulsion? Zounds, and I were at the strappado or all the racks in the world, I would not tell you on compulsion. Give you a reason on compulsion? If reasons were as plentiful as blackberries, I would give no man a reason upon compulsion, I.

Prince. I'll be no longer guilty of this sin; this sanguine coward, this bed-presser, this horseback-breaker, this huge hill of flesh—

Falstaff. 'Sblood, you starveling, you eel-skin, you dried neat's-tongue, you bull's pizzle, you stockfish—O for breath to utter what is like thee!—you tailor's yard, you sheath, you bowcase, you vile standing tuck!

Prince. Well, breathe awhile, and then to it again; and when thou hast tired thyself in base comparisons, hear me speak but this.

Poins. Mark, Jack.

Prince. We two saw you four set on four, and bound them and were masters of their wealth. Mark now how a plain tale shall put you down. Then did we two set on you four and, with a word, outfaced you from your prize, and have it; yea, and can show it you here in the house. And, Falstaff, you carried your guts away as nimbly, with as quick dexterity, and roared for mercy, and still run and roared, as ever I heard bullcalf. What a slave art thou to hack thy sword as thou hast done, and then say it was in fight! What trick, what device, what starting hole canst thou now find out to hide thee from this open and apparent shame?

Poins. Come, let's hear, Jack. What trick hast thou now?

Falstaff. I knew ye as well as he that made ye. Why, hear you, my masters. Was it for me to kill the heir apparent? Should I turn upon the true prince? Why, thou knowest I am as valiant as Hercules, but beware instinct. The lion will not touch the true prince. Instinct is a great matter. I was now a coward on instinct. I shall think the better of myself, and thee, during my life—I for a valiant lion, and thou for a true prince. But, by the Lord, lads, I am glad you have the money. Hostess, clap to the doors. Watch tonight, pray tomorrow. Gallants, lads, boys, hearts of gold, all the titles of good fellowship come to you! What, shall we be merry? Shall we have a play extempore?

Prince. Content—and the argument shall be thy running away.

Falstaff. Ah, no more of that, Hal, and thou lovest me!

[Enter Hostess]

Hostess. My lord the Prince!

Prince. How now, my lady the hostess? What say'st thou to me?

Hostess. Marry, my lord, there is a nobleman of the court at door would speak with you. He says he comes from your father.

Prince. Give him as much as will make him a royal man, and send him back again to my mother.

Falstaff.	What manner of man is he?
Hostess.	An old man.
Falstaff.	What doth gravity out of his bed at midnight? Shall I give him his answer?
Prince.	Prithee do, Jack.
Falstaff.	Faith, and I'll send him packing.

[*Exit*]

Prince. Now, sirs. By'r Lady, you fought fair; so did you, Peto; so did you, Bardolph. You are lions too, you ran away upon instinct, you will not touch the true prince; no—fie!

Bardolph. Faith, I ran when I saw others run.

Prince. Faith, tell me now in earnest, how came Falstaff's sword so hacked?

Peto. Why, he hacked it with his dagger, and said he would swear truth out of England but he would make you believe it was done in fight, and persuaded us to do the like.

Bardolph. Yea, and to tickle our noses with speargrass to make them bleed, and then to beslubber our garments with it and swear it was the blood of true men. I did that I did not this seven year before—I blushed to hear his monstrous devices.

Prince. O villain! Thou stolest a cup of sack eighteen years ago and wert taken with the manner, and ever since thou hast blushed extempore. Thou hadst fire and sword on thy side, and yet thou ran'st away. What instinct hadst thou for it?

Bardolph. My lord, do you see these meteors? Do you behold these exhalations?

Prince. I do.

Bardolph. What think you they portend?

Prince. Hot livers and cold purses.

Bardolph. Choler, my lord, if rightly taken.

Prince. No, if rightly taken, halter.

[*Enter Falstaff*]

Here comes lean Jack; here comes bare-bone. How now, my sweet creature of bombast? How long is't ago, Jack, since thou sawest thine own knee?

Falstaff.	My own knee? When I was about thy years, Hal, I was not an eagle's talent in the waist; I could have crept into any alderman's thumb-ring. A plague of sighing and grief, it blows a man up like a bladder. There's villainous news abroad. Here was Sir John Bracy from your father: you must to the court in the morning. That same mad fellow of the north, Percy, and he of Wales that gave Amamon the bastinado, and made Lucifer cuckold, and swore the devil his true liegeman upon the cross of a Welsh hook—what a plague call you him?
Poins.	Owen Glendower.
Falstaff.	Owen, Owen—the same; and his son-in-law Mortimer, and old Northumberland, and that sprightly Scot of Scots, Douglas, that runs a-horseback up a hill perpendicular—
Prince.	He that rides at high speed and with his pistol kills a sparrow flying.
Falstaff.	You have hit it.
Prince.	So did he never the sparrow.
Falstaff.	Well, that rascal hath good metal in him; he will not run.
Prince.	Why, what a rascal art thou then, to praise him so for running!
Falstaff.	A-horseback, ye cuckoo! But afoot he will not budge a foot.
Prince.	Yes, Jack, upon instinct.
Falstaff.	I grant ye, upon instinct. Well, he is there too, and one Mordake, and a thousand bluecaps more. Worcester is stol'n away tonight; thy father's beard is turned white with the news; you may buy land now as cheap as stinking mack'rel.
Prince.	Why then, it is like, if there come a hot June, and this civil buffeting hold, we shall buy maidenheads as they buy hobnails, by the hundreds.

Falstaff. By the mass, lad, thou sayest true; it is like we shall have good trading that way. But tell me, Hal, art not thou horrible afeard? Thou being heir apparent, could the world pick thee out three such enemies again as that fiend Douglas, that spirit Percy, and that devil Glendower? Art thou not horribly afraid? Doth not thy blood thrill at it?

Prince. Not a whit, i' faith. I lack some of thy instinct.

Falstaff. Well, thou wilt be horribly chid tomorrow when thou comest to thy father. If thou love me, practice an answer.

Prince. Do thou stand for my father and examine me upon the particulars of my life.

Falstaff. Shall I? Content. This chair shall be my state, this dagger my scepter, and this cushion my crown.

Prince. Thy state is taken for a joined-stool, thy golden scepter for a leaden dagger, and thy precious rich crown for a pitiful bald crown.

Falstaff. Well, and the fire of grace be not quite out of thee, now shalt thou be moved. Give me a cup of sack to make my eyes look red, that it may be thought I have wept; for I must speak in passion, and I will do it in King Cambyses' vein.

Prince. Well, here is my leg.

Falstaff. And here is my speech. Stand aside, nobility.

Hostess. O Jesu, this excellent sport, i' faith!

Falstaff. Weep not, sweet queen, for trickling tears are vain.

Hostess. O, the Father, how he holds his countenance!

Falstaff. For God's sake, lords, convey my tristful queen!
For tears do stop the floodgates of her eyes.

Hostess. O Jesu, he doth it as like one of these harlotry players as ever I see!

Falstaff. Peace, good pintpot. Peace, good tickle-brain. Harry, I do not only marvel where thou spendest thy time, but also how thou art accompanied. For though the camomile, the more it is trodden on, the faster it grows, so youth, the more it is wasted, the sooner it wears. That thou art my son I have partly thy mother's word, partly my own opinion, but chiefly a villainous trick of thine eye and a foolish hanging of thy nether lip that doth warrant me. If then thou be son to me, here lies the point: why, being son to me, art thou so pointed at? Shall the blessed sun of heaven prove a micher and eat blackberries? A question not to be asked. Shall the son of England prove a thief and take purses? A question to be asked. There is a thing, Harry, which thou hast often heard of, and it is known to many in our land by the name of pitch. This pitch (as ancient writers do report) doth defile; so doth the company thou keepest. For, Harry, now I do not speak to thee in drink, but in tears; not in pleasure, but in passion; not in words only, but in woes also: and yet there is a virtuous man whom I have often noted in thy company, but I know not his name.

Prince. What manner of man, and it like your Majesty?

Falstaff. A goodly portly man, i' faith, and a corpulent; of a cheerful look, a pleasing eye, and a most noble carriage; and, as I think, his age some fifty, or, by'r Lady, inclining to threescore; and now I remember me, his name is Falstaff. If that man should be lewdly given, he deceiveth me; for, Harry, I see virtue in his looks. If then the tree may be known by the fruit, as the fruit by the tree, then, peremptorily I speak it, there is virtue in that Falstaff. Him keep with, the rest banish. And tell me now, thou naughty varlet, tell me where hast thou been this month?

Prince. Dost thou speak like a king? Do thou stand for me, and I'll play my father.

Falstaff. Depose me? If thou dost it half so gravely, so majestically, both in word and matter, hang me up by the heels for a rabbit-sucker or a poulter's hare.

Prince. Well, here I am set.

Falstaff.	And here I stand. Judge, my masters.
Prince.	Now, Harry, whence come you?
Falstaff.	My noble lord, from Eastcheap.
Prince.	The complaints I hear of thee are grievous.
Falstaff.	'Sblood, my lord, they are false! Nay, I'll tickle ye for a young prince, i' faith.
Prince.	Swearest thou, ungracious boy? Henceforth ne'er look on me. Thou art violently carried away from grace. There is a devil haunts thee in the likeness of an old fat man; a tun of man is thy companion. Why dost thou converse with that trunk of humors, that bolting-hutch of beastliness, that swoll'n parcel of dropsies, that huge bombard of sack, that stuffed cloakbag of guts, that roasted Manningtree ox with the pudding in his belly, that reverend vice, that gray iniquity, that father ruffian, that vanity in years? Wherein is he good, but to taste sack and drink it? Wherein neat and cleanly, but to carve a capon and eat it? Wherein cunning, but in craft? Wherein crafty, but in villainy? Wherein villainous, but in all things? Wherein worthy, but in nothing?
Falstaff.	I would your Grace would take me with you. Whom means your Grace?
Prince.	That villainous abominable misleader of youth, Falstaff, that old white-bearded Satan.
Falstaff.	My lord, the man I know.
Prince.	I know thou dost.
Falstaff.	But to say I know more harm in him than in myself were to say more than I know. That he is old, the more the pity, his white hairs do witness it; but that he is, saving your reverence, a whoremaster, that I utterly deny. If sack and sugar be a fault, God help the wicked! If to be old and merry be a sin, then many an old host that I know is damned. If to be fat be to be hated, then Pharaoh's lean kine are to be loved. No, my good lord: banish Peto, banish Bardolph, banish Poins; but for sweet Jack Falstaff, kind Jack Falstaff, true Jack Falstaff, valiant Jack Falstaff, and therefore more valiant being, as he is, old Jack Falstaff, banish not him thy Harry's company, banish not him thy Harry's company, banish plump Jack, and banish all the world!

Prince.	I do, I will. [*A knocking heard*]
	[*Exeunt the Hostess, with Francis, and* *Bardolph. Reenter Bardolph, running*]
Bardolph.	O, my lord, my lord! The sheriff with a most, most monstrous watch is at the door.
Falstaff.	Out, ye rogue! Play out the play, I have much to say in the behalf of that Falstaff.
	[*Enter the Hostess*]
Hostess.	O Jesu, my lord, my lord!
Prince.	Heigh, heigh, the devil rides upon a fiddlestick! What's the matter?
Hostess.	The sheriff and all the watch are at the door. They are come to search the house. Shall I let them in?
Falstaff.	Dost thou hear, Hal? Never call a true piece of gold a counterfeit. Thou art essentially made without seeming so.
Prince.	And thou a natural coward without instinct.
Falstaff.	I deny your major. If you will deny the sheriff, so; if not, let him enter. If I become not a cart as well as another man, a plague on my bringing up! I hope I shall as soon be strangled with a halter as another.
Prince.	Go hide thee behind the arras. The rest walk up above. Now, my masters, for a true face and good conscience.
Falstaff.	Both which I have had; but their date is out, and therefore I'll hide me. [*Exit*]
Prince.	Call in the sheriff.
	[*Exeunt all but Prince Henry and* *Peto. Enter Sheriff and the Carrier*]
	Now, master sheriff, what is your will with me?
Sheriff.	First, pardon me, my lord. A hue and cry hath followed certain men unto this house.
Prince.	What men?
Sheriff.	One of them is well known, my gracious lord—a gross fat man.
Carrier.	As fat as butter.

Prince.	The man, I do assure you, is not here,
	For I myself at this time have employed him.
	And, sheriff, I will engage my word to thee
	That I will by tomorrow dinner time
	Send him to answer thee, or any man,
	For anything he shall be charged withal;
	And so let me entreat you leave the house.
Sheriff.	I will, my lord. There are two gentlemen
	Have in this robbery lost three hundred marks.
Prince.	It may be so. If he have robbed these men,
	He shall be answerable; and so farewell.
Sheriff.	Good night, my noble lord.
Prince.	I think it is good morrow, is it not?
Sheriff.	Indeed, my lord, I think it be two o'clock.

      [Exit with Carrier]

Prince.	This oily rascal is known as well as Paul's. Go call him forth.
Peto.	Falstaff! Fast asleep behind the arras, and snorting like a horse.
Prince.	Hark how hard he fetches breath. Search his pockets.

      [He searches his pockets and finds certain papers]

	What hast thou found?
Peto.	Nothing but papers, my lord.
Prince.	Let's see what they be. Read them.

Peto.   *[Reading]*
                "*Item, A capon* . . . . *2s. 2d.*
                Item, Sauce . . . . *4d.*
                Item, Sack two gallons . . . . *5s. 8d.*
                Item, Anchovies and sack after supper . . . . *2s. 6d.*
                Item, Bread . . . . *ob.*"

Prince. O monstrous! But one halfpennyworth of bread to this intolerable deal of sack! What there is else, keep close; we'll read it at more advantage. There let him sleep till day. I'll to the court in the morning. We must all to the wars, and thy place shall be honorable. I'll procure this fat rogue a charge of foot, and I know his death will be a march of twelve score. The money shall be paid back again with advantage. Be with me betimes in the morning, and so good morrow, Peto.

Peto. Good morrow, good my lord.

        [Exeunt]

PART I ACT THREE

*[Enter Hotspur, Worcester, the Lord
Mortimer and Owen Glendower]*

Mortimer.　These promises are fair, the parties sure,

And our induction full of prosperous hope.

Hotspur.　Lord Mortimer, and cousin Glendower,

Will you sit down?

And uncle Worcester;

A plague upon it.

I have forgot the map.

Glendower.　No, here it is.

Sit, cousin Percy, sit, good cousin Hotspur,

For by that name as oft as Lancaster doth speak of you,

His cheek looks pale, and with a rising sigh

He wisheth you in heaven.

Hotspur.　　　　　　　　　　And you in hell,

As oft as he hears Owen Glendower spoke of.

Glendower.　I cannot blame him. At my nativity

The front of heaven was full of fiery shapes

Of burning cressets, and at my birth

The frame and huge foundation of the earth

Shaked like a coward.

Hotspur.　Why, so it would have done at the same season

If your mother's cat had but kittened,

Though yourself had never been born.

Glendower.　I say the earth did shake when I was born.

Hotspur.	And I say the earth was not of my mind,
	If you suppose as fearing you it shook.
Glendower.	The heavens were all on fire, the earth did tremble.
Hotspur.	O, then the earth shook to see the heavens on fire,
	And not in fear of your nativity.
	Diseased nature oftentimes breaks forth
	In strange eruptions; oft the teeming earth
	Is with a kind of colic pinched and vexed
	By the imprisoning of unruly wind
	Within her womb, which, for enlargement striving,
	Shakes the old beldame earth and topples down
	Steeples and mossgrown towers. At your birth
	Our grandam earth, having this distemp'rature,
	In passion shook.
Glendower.	Cousin, of many men
	I do not bear these crossings. Give me leave
	To tell you once again that at my birth
	The front of heaven was full of fiery shapes,
	The goats ran from the mountains, and the herds
	Were strangely clamorous to the frighted fields.
	These signs have marked me extraordinary,
	And all the courses of my life do show
	I am not in the roll of common men.
	Where is he living, clipped in with the sea
	That chides the banks of England, Scotland, Wales,
	Which calls me pupil or hath read to me?

And bring him out that is but woman's son
Can trace me in the tedious ways of art
And hold me pace in deep experiments.

Hotspur. I think there's no man speaks better Welsh.
I'll to dinner.

Mortimer. Peace, cousin Percy; you will make him mad.

Glendower. I can call spirits from the vasty deep.

Hotspur. Why, so can I, or so can any man;
But will they come when you do call for them?

Glendower. Why, I can teach you, cousin, to command the devil.

Hotspur. And I can teach thee, coz, to shame the devil—
By telling truth. Tell truth and shame the devil.
If thou have power to raise him, bring him hither,
And I'll be sworn I have power to shame him hence.
O, while you live, tell truth and shame the devil!

Mortimer. Come, come, no more of this unprofitable chat.

Glendower. Three times hath Henry Bolingbroke made head
Against my power; thrice from the banks of Wye
And sandy-bottomed Severn have I sent him
Booteless home and weather-beaten back.

Hotspur. Home without boots, and in foul weather too?
How scapes he agues, in the devil's name?

Glendower. Come, here's the map. Shall we divide our right
According to our threefold order ta'en?

Mortimer.   The Archdeacon hath divided it
          Into three limits very equally.
          England, from Trent and Severn hitherto,
          By south and east is to my part assigned;
          All westward, Wales beyond the Severn shore,
          And all the fertile land within that bound,
          To Owen Glendower; and, dear coz, to you
          The remnant northward lying off from Trent.
          And our indentures tripartite are drawn,
          Which being sealed interchangeably
          (A business that this night may execute),
          Tomorrow, cousin Percy, you and I
          And my good Lord of Worcester will set forth
          To meet your father and the Scottish power,
          As is appointed us, at Shrewsbury.
          My father Glendower is not ready yet,
          Nor shall we need his help these fourteen days.
                [*To Glendower*]
          Within that space you may have drawn together
          Your tenants, friends, and neighboring gentlemen.
Glendower.   A shorter time shall send me to you, lords;
          And in my conduct shall your ladies come,
          From whom you now must steal and take no leave,
          For there will be a world of water shed
          Upon the parting of your wives and you.

Hotspur.	Methinks my moiety, north from Burton here,
	In quantity equals not one of yours.
	See how this river comes me cranking in
	And cuts me from the best of all my land
	A huge half-moon, a monstrous cantle out.
	I'll have the current in this place dammed up,
	And here the smug and silver Trent shall run
	In a new channel fair and evenly.
	It shall not wind with such a deep indent
	To rob me of so rich a bottom here.
Glendower.	Not wind? It shall, it must! You see it doth.
Mortimer.	Yea, but mark how he bears his course,
	And runs me up with like advantage on the other side,
	Gelding the opposed continent as much
	As on the other side it takes from you.
Worcester.	Yea, but a little charge will trench him here
	And on this north side win this cape of land;
	And then he runs straight and even.
Hotspur.	I'll have it so, a little charge will do it.
Glendower.	I'll not have it alt'red.
Hotspur.	Will not you?
Glendower.	No, nor you shall not.
Hotspur.	Who shall say me nay?
Glendower.	Why, that will I.
Hotspur.	Let me not understand you then; speak it in Welsh.

Glendower.	I can speak English, lord, as well as you;
	For I was trained up in the English court,
	Where, being but young, I framed to the harp
	Many an English ditty lovely well,
	And gave the tongue a helpful ornament —
	A virtue that was never seen in you.
Hotspur.	Marry, and I am glad of it with all my heart!
	I had rather be a kitten and cry mew
	Than one of these same meter ballad-mongers.
	I had rather hear a brazen canstick turned
	Or a dry wheel grate on the axletree,
	And that would set my teeth nothing on edge,
	Nothing so much as mincing poetry.
	Tis like the forced gait of a shuffling nag.
Glendower.	Come, you shall have Trent turned.
Hotspur.	I do not care. I'll give thrice so much land
	To any well-deserving friend;
	But in the way of bargain, mark ye me,
	I'll cavil on the ninth part of a hair.
	Are the indentures drawn? Shall we be gone?
Glendower.	The moon shines fair;
	You may away by night.
	I'll haste the writer, and withal
	Break with your wives of your departure hence.
	I am afraid my daughter will run mad,
	So much she doteth on her Mortimer. [*Exit*]
Mortimer.	Fie, cousin Percy, how you cross my father!

Hotspur. I cannot choose. Sometime he angers me
With telling me of the moldwarp and the ant,
Of the dreamer Merlin and his prophecies,
And of a dragon and a finless fish,
A clip-winged griffin and a moulten raven,
A couching lion and a ramping cat,
And such a deal of skimble-skamble stuff
As puts me from my faith. I tell you what—
He held me last night at least nine hours
In reckoning up the several devils' names
That were his lackeys. I cried "hum," and "Well, go to!"
But marked him not a word. O, he is as tedious
As a tired horse, a railing wife;
Worse than a smoky house. I had rather live
With cheese and garlic in a windmill far
Than feed on cates and have him talk to me
In any summer house in Christendom.

Mortimer. In faith, he is a worthy gentleman,
Exceedingly well read and profited
In strange concealments, valiant as a lion,
And wondrous affable, and as bountiful
As mines of India. Shall I tell you, cousin?
He holds your temper in a high respect
And curbs himself even of his natural scope
When you come 'cross his humor. Faith, he does.
I warrant you that man is not alive
Might so have tempted him as you have done
Without the taste of danger and reproof.
But do not use it oft, let me entreat you.

Worcester. In faith, my lord, you are too willful-blame,
And since your coming hither have done enough
To put him quite besides his patience.
You must needs learn, lord, to amend this fault.
Though sometimes it show greatness, courage, blood —
And that's the dearest grace it renders you —
Yet oftentimes it doth present harsh rage,
Defect of manners, want of government,
Pride, haughtiness, opinion, and disdain;
The least of which haunting a nobleman
Loseth men's hearts, and leaves behind a stain
Upon the beauty of all parts besides,
Beguiling them of commendation.

Hotspur.	Well, I am schooled. Good manners be your speed!
	Here come our wives, and let us take our leave.

[Enter Glendower with the Ladies]

Mortimer.	This is the deadly spite that angers me —
	My wife can speak no English, I no Welsh.
Glendower.	My daughter weeps; she'll not part with you,
	She'll be a soldier too, she'll to the wars.
Mortimer.	Good father, tell her that she and my aunt Percy
	Shall follow in your conduct speedily.

[Glendower speaks to her in Welsh,
and she answers him in the same]

Glendower.	She is desperate here.
	A peevish self-willed harlotry,
	One that no persuasion can do good upon.

[The Lady speaks in Welsh]

Mortimer.	I understand thy looks. That pretty Welsh
	Which thou pourest down from these swelling heavens
	I am too perfect in; and, but for shame,
	In such a parley should I answer thee.

[The Lady again in Welsh]

I understand thy kisses, and thou mine,
And that's a feeling disputation.
But I will never be a truant, love,
Till I have learnt thy language; for thy tongue
Makes Welsh as sweet as ditties highly penned,
Sung by a fair queen in a summer's bow'r,
With ravishing division, to her lute.

Glendower.	Nay, if you melt, then will she run mad.
	[The Lady speaks again in Welsh]
Mortimer.	O, I am ignorance itself in this!
Glendower.	She bids you on the wanton rushes lay you down
	And rest your gentle head upon her lap,
	And she will sing the song that pleaseth you
	And on your eyelids crown the god of sleep,
	Charming your blood with pleasing heaviness,
	Making such difference 'twixt wake and sleep
	As is the difference betwixt day and night
	The hour before the heavenly-harnessed team
	Begins his golden progress in the east.
Mortimer.	With all my heart I'll sit and hear her sing.
	By that time will our book, I think, be drawn.
Glendower.	Do so, and those musicians that shall play to you
	Hang in the air a thousand leagues from hence,
	And straight they shall be here: sit, and attend.
Hotspur.	Come, Kate, thou art perfect in lying down.
	Come, quick, quick, that I may lay my head in thy lap.
Lady Percy.	Go, ye giddy goose. *[The music plays]*
Hotspur.	Now I perceive the devil understands Welsh,
	And 'tis no marvel he is so humorous,
	By'r Lady, he is a good musician.

Lady Percy.	Then should you be nothing but musical,
	For you are altogether governed by humors.
	Lie still, ye thief, and hear the lady sing in Welsh.
Hotspur.	I had rather hear Lady, my brach, howl in Irish.
Lady Percy.	Wouldst thou have thy head broken?
Hotspur.	No.
Lady Percy.	Then be still.
Hotspur.	Neither! 'Tis a woman's fault.
Lady Percy.	Now God help thee!
Hotspur.	To the Welsh lady's bed.
Lady Percy.	What's that?
Hotspur.	Peace! She sings. [*Here the Lady sings a Welsh song*]
	Come, Kate, I'll have your song too.
Lady Percy.	Not mine, in good sooth.
Hotspur.	Not yours, in good sooth?
	You swear like a comfit-maker's wife:
	Not you, in good sooth; and, as true as I live;
	And, as God shall mend me; and, as sure as day:
	And givest such sarcenet surety for thy oaths
	As if thou never walk'st further than Finsbury.
	Swear me, Kate, like a lady as thou art,
	A good mouth-filling oath, and leave in sooth
	And such protest of pepper gingerbread
	To velvet guards and Sunday citizens.
	Come, sing.

Lady Percy.	I will not sing.
Hotspur.	'Tis the next way to turn tailor or be red-breast-teacher.
	And the indentures be drawn, I'll away within these two hours;
	And so come in when ye will.
	[*Exit*]
Glendower.	Come, come, Lord Mortimer. You are as slow
	As hot Lord Percy is on fire to go.
	By this our book is drawn; we'll but seal,
	And then to horse immediately.
Mortimer.	With all my heart.
	[*Exeunt*]

[Enter the King, Prince of Wales, and others]

King. Lords, give us leave:

The Prince of Wales, and I,

Must have some private conference;

But be near at hand,

For we shall presently have need of you.

    [Exeunt Lords]

I know not whether God will have it so

For some displeasing service I have done,

That, in his secret doom, out of my blood

He'll breed revengement and a scourge for me;

But thou dost in thy passages of life

Make me believe that thou art only marked

For the hot vengeance and the rod of heaven

To punish my mistreadings. Tell me else,

Could such inordinate and low desires,

Such poor, such bare, such lewd, such mean attempts,

Such barren pleasures, rude society,

As thou art matched withal and grafted to,

Accompany the greatness of thy blood

And hold their level with thy princely heart?

Prince. So please your Majesty, I would I could

Quit all offenses with as clear excuse

As well as I am doubtless I can purge

Myself of many I am charged withal.

Yet such extenuation let me beg
As, in reproof of many tales devised,
Which oft the ear of greatness needs must hear
By smiling pickthanks and base newsmongers,
I may, for some things true wherein my youth
Hath faulty wand'red and irregular,
Find pardon on my true submission.

King.   God pardon thee! Yet let me wonder, Harry,
At thy affections, which do hold a wing
Quite from the flight of all thy ancestors.
Thy place in council thou hast rudely lost,
Which by thy younger brother is supplied,
And art almost an alien to the hearts
Of all the court and princes of my blood.
The hope and expectation of thy time
Is ruined, and the soul of every man
Prophetically do forethink thy fall.
Had I so lavish of my presence been,
So common-hackneyed in the eyes of men,
So stale and cheap to vulgar company,
Opinion, that did help me to the crown,
Had still kept loyal to possession
And left me in reputeless banishment,
A fellow of no mark nor likelihood.
By being seldom seen, I could not stir
But, like a comet, I was wond'red at;
That men would tell their children, "This is he!"

Others would say, "Where? Which is Bolingbroke?"
And then I stole all courtesy from heaven,
And dressed myself in such humility
That I did pluck allegiance from men's hearts,
Loud shouts and salutations from their mouths
Even in the presence of the crowned King.
Thus did I keep my person fresh and new,
My presence, like a robe pontifical,
Ne'er seen but wond'red at; and so my state,
Seldom but sumptuous, showed like a feast
And won by rareness such solemnity.
The skipping King, he ambled up and down
With shallow jesters and rash bavin wits,
Soon kindled and soon burnt; carded his state;
Mingled his royalty with cap'ring fools;
Had his great name profaned with their scorns
And gave his countenance, against his name,
To laugh at gibing boys and stand the push
Of every beardless vain comparative;
Grew a companion to the common streets,
Enfeoffed himself to popularity;
That, being daily swallowed by men's eyes,
They surfeited with honey and began
To loathe the taste of sweetness, whereof a little
More than a little is by much too much.
So, when he had occasion to be seen,
He was but as the cuckoo is in June,

Heard, not regarded—seen, but with such eyes
As, sick and blunted with community,
Afford no extraordinary gaze,
Such as is bent on sunlike majesty
When it shines seldom in admiring eyes;
But rather drowsed and hung their eyelids down,
Slept in his face, and rend'red such aspect
As cloudy men use to their adversaries,
Being with his presence glutted, gorged, and full.
And in that very line, Harry, standest thou;
For thou hast lost thy princely privilege
With vile participation. Not an eye
But is aweary of thy common sight,
Save mine, which hath desired to see thee more;
Which now doth that I would not have it do—
Make blind itself with foolish tenderness.

Prince. I shall hereafter, my thrice-gracious lord,
Be more myself.

King.   For all the world,
As thou art to this hour was Richard then
When I from France set foot at Ravenspurgh;
And even as I was then is Percy now.
Now, by my scepter, and my soul to boot,
He hath more worthy interest to the state
Than thou the shadow of succession;
For of no right, nor color like to right,
He doth fill fields with harness in the realm,

Turns head against the lion's armed jaws,
And, being no more in debt to years than thou,
Leads ancient lords and reverend bishops on
To bloody battles and to bruising arms.
What never-dying honor hath he got
Against renowned Douglas! whose high deeds,
Whose hot incursions and great name in arms
Holds from all soldiers chief majority
And military title capital
Through all the kingdoms that acknowledge Christ.
Thrice hath this Hotspur, Mars in swathling clothes,
This infant warrior, in his enterprises
Discomfited great Douglas; ta'en him once,
Enlarged him, and made a friend of him,
To fill the mouth of deep defiance up
And shake the peace and safety of our throne.
And what say you to this? Percy, Northumberland,
The Archbishop's grace of York, Douglas, Mortimer
Capitulate against us and are up.
But wherefore do I tell these news to thee?
Why, Harry, do I tell thee of my foes,
Which art my nearest and dearest enemy?
Thou that art like enough, through vassal fear,
Base inclination, and the start of spleen,
To fight against me under Percy's pay,
To dog his heels and curtsy at his frowns,
To show how much thou art degenerate.

Prince. Do not think so, you shall not find it so.
And God forgive them that so much have swayed
Your Majesty's good thoughts away from me.
I will redeem all this on Percy's head
And, in the closing of some glorious day,
Be bold to tell you that I am your son,
When I will wear a garment all of blood,
And stain my favors in a bloody mask,
Which, washed away, shall scour my shame with it.
And that shall be the day, whene'er it lights,
That this same child of honor and renown,
This gallant Hotspur, this all-praised knight,
And your unthought-of Harry chance to meet.
For every honor sitting on his helm,
Would they were multitudes, and on my head
My shames redoubled! For the time will come
That I shall make this northern youth exchange
His glorious deeds for my indignities.
Percy is but my factor, good my lord,
To engross up glorious deeds on my behalf;
And I will call him to so strict account
That he shall render every glory up,
Yea, even the slightest worship of his time,
Or I will tear the reckoning from his heart.
This in the name of God I promise here;
The which if he be pleased I shall perform,
I do beseech your Majesty may salve

The long-grown wounds of my intemperance.
If not, the end of life cancels all bands,
And I will die a hundred thousand deaths
Ere break the smallest parcel of this vow.

King. A hundred thousand rebels die in this!
Thou shalt have charge and sovereign trust herein.
[Enter Blunt]
How now, good Blunt? Thy looks are full of speed.

Blunt. So hath the business that I come to speak of.
Lord Mortimer of Scotland hath sent word
That Douglas and the English rebels met
The eleventh of this month at Shrewsbury.
A mighty and a fearful head they are,
If promises be kept on every hand,
As ever off'red foul play in a state.

King. The Earl of Westmoreland set forth today;
With him my son, Lord John of Lancaster:
For this advertisement is five days old.
On Wednesday next, Harry, you shall set forward;
On Thursday we ourselves will march. Our meeting
Is Bridgenorth; and, Harry, you shall march
Through Gloucestershire; by which account,
Our business valued, some twelve days hence
Our general forces at Bridgenorth shall meet.
Our hands are full of business. Let's away:
Advantage feeds him fat while men delay.
[Exeunt]

[Enter Falstaff and Bardolph]

Falstaff.   Bardolph, am I not fall'n away vilely since this last action? Do I not bate? Do I
not dwindle? Why, my skin hangs about me like an old lady's loose gown! I am
withered like an old apple-john. Well, I'll repent, and that suddenly, while I am
in some liking. I shall be out of heart shortly, and then I shall have no strength to
repent. And I have not forgotten what the inside of a church is made of, I am a
peppercorn, a brewer's horse. The inside of a church! Company, villainous
company, hath been the spoil of me.

Bardolph.   Sir John, you are so fretful you cannot live long.

Falstaff.   Why, there is it! Come, sing me a bawdy song, make me merry. I was as virtuously
given as a gentleman need to be, virtuous enough: swore little, diced not above
seven times a week, went to a bawdy house not above once in a quarter of an
hour, paid money that I borrowed three or four times, lived well, and in good
compass; and now I live out of all order, out of all compass.

Bardolph.   Why, you are so fat, Sir John, that you must needs be out of all compass—out of
all reasonable compass, Sir John.

Falstaff.   Do thou amend thy face, and I'll amend my life. Thou art our admiral, thou
bearest the lantern in the poop—but 'tis in the nose of thee: thou art the Knight
of the Burning Lamp.

Bardolph.   Why, Sir John, my face does you no harm.

Falstaff.   No, I'll be sworn. I make as good use of it as many a man doth of a death's-head
or a memento mori. I never see thy face but I think upon hellfire and Dives that
lived in purple; for there he is in his robes, burning, burning. If thou wert any
way given to virtue, I would swear by thy face; my oath should be "By this fire,
that's God's angel." But thou art altogether given over, and wert indeed, but for

the light in thy face, the son of utter darkness. When thou ran'st up Gad's Hill in the night to catch my horse, if I did not think thou hadst been an ignis fatuus or a ball of wildfire, there's no purchase in money. O, thou art a perpetual triumph, an everlasting bonfire-light! Thou hast saved me a thousand marks in links and torches, walking with thee in the night betwixt tavern and tavern; but the sack that thou hast drunk me would have bought me lights as good cheap at the dearest chandler's in Europe. I have maintained that salamander of yours with fire any time this two and thirty years. God reward me for it!

Bardolph. 'Sblood, I would my face were in your belly!

Falstaff. God-a-mercy! So should I be sure to be heartburned.

[Enter Hostess]

How now, Dame Partlet the hen? Have you enquired yet who picked my pocket?

Hostess. Why, Sir John, what do you think, Sir John? Do you think I keep thieves in my house? I have searched, I have enquired, so has my husband, man by man, boy by boy, servant by servant. The tithe of a hair was never lost in my house before.

Falstaff. Ye lie, hostess. Bardolph was shaved and lost many a hair, and I'll be sworn my pocket was picked. Go to, you are a woman, go!

Hostess. Who, I? No; I defy thee! God's light, I was never called so in mine own house before!

Falstaff. Go to, I know you well enough.

Hostess. No, Sir John; you do not know me, Sir John. I know you, Sir John. You owe me money, Sir John, and now you pick a quarrel to beguile me of it. I bought you a dozen of shirts to your back.

Falstaff. Dowlas, filthy dowlas! I have given them away to bakers' wives; they have made bolters of them.

Hostess. Now, as I am a true woman, holland of eight shillings an ell. You owe money here besides, Sir John, for your diet and by-drinkings, and money lent you, four and twenty pound.

Falstaff. He had his part of it; let him pay.

Hostess.	He? Alas, he is poor; he hath nothing.
Falstaff.	How? Poor? Look upon his face. What call you rich? Let them coin his nose, let them coin his cheeks. I'll not pay a denier. What, will you make a younker of me? Shall I not take mine ease in mine inn but I shall have my pocket picked? I have lost a seal ring of my grandfather's worth forty mark.
Hostess.	O Jesu, I have heard the Prince tell him, I know not how oft, that that ring was copper!
Falstaff.	How? The Prince is a Jack, a sneak-up. 'Sblood, and he were here, I would cudgel him like a dog if he would say so.

[*Enter the Prince and Poins, marching. Falstaff meets them both, playing upon his truncheon like a fife*]

How now, lad? Is the wind in that door, i' faith? Must we all march?

Bardolph.	Yea, two and two, Newgate fashion.
Hostess.	My lord, I pray you hear me.
Prince.	What say'st thou, Mistress Quickly? How doth thy husband? I love him well, he is an honest man.
Hostess.	Good my lord, hear me.
Falstaff.	Prithee let her alone and list to me.
Prince.	What say'st thou, Jack?
Falstaff.	The other night I fell asleep here behind the arras and had my pocket picked. This house is turned bawdy house; they pick pockets.
Prince.	What didst thou lose, Jack?
Falstaff.	Wilt thou believe me, Hal, three or four bonds of forty pound apiece and a seal ring of my grandfather's.
Prince.	A trifle, some eightpenny matter.
Hostess.	So I told him, my lord, and I said I heard your Grace say so; and, my lord, he speaks most vilely of you, like a foulmouthed man as he is, and said he would cudgel you.
Prince.	What! He did not?

Hostess.	There's neither faith, truth, nor womanhood in me else.
Falstaff.	There's no more faith in thee than in a stewed prune, nor no more truth in thee than in a drawn fox; and for womanhood, Maid Marian may be the deputy's wife of the ward to thee. Go, you thing, go!
Hostess.	Say, what thing, what thing?
Falstaff.	What thing? Why, a thing to thank God on.
Hostess.	I am no thing to thank God on, I would thou shouldst know it! I am an honest man's wife, and, setting thy knighthood aside, thou art a knave to call me so.
Falstaff.	Setting thy womanhood aside, thou art a beast to say otherwise.
Hostess.	Say, what beast, thou knave, thou?
Falstaff.	What beast? Why, an otter.
Prince.	An otter, Sir John? Why an otter?
Falstaff.	Why, she's neither fish nor flesh; a man knows not where to have her.
Hostess.	Thou art an unjust man in saying so. Thou or any man knows where to have me, thou knave, thou!
Prince.	Thou say'st true, hostess, and he slanders thee most grossly.
Hostess.	So he doth you, my lord, and said this other day you ought him a thousand pound.
Prince.	Sirrah, do I owe you a thousand pound?
Falstaff.	A thousand pound, Hal? A million! Thy love is worth a million, thou owest me thy love.
Hostess.	Nay, my lord, he called you Jack and said he would cudgel you.
Falstaff.	Did I, Bardolph?
Bardolph.	Indeed, Sir John, you said so.
Falstaff.	Yea, if he said my ring was copper.
Prince.	I say 'tis copper. Darest thou be as good as thy word now?
Falstaff.	Why, Hal, thou knowest, as thou art but man, I dare; but as thou art Prince, I fear thee as I fear the roaring of the lion's whelp.
Prince.	And why not as the lion?

Falstaff.	The King himself is to be feared as the lion. Dost thou think I'll fear thee as I fear thy father? Nay, and I do, I pray God my girdle break.
Prince.	O, if it should, how would thy guts fall about thy knees! But, sirrah, there's no room for faith, truth, nor honesty in this bosom of thine. It is all filled up with guts and midriff. Charge an honest woman with picking thy pocket? Why, thou whoreson, impudent, embossed rascal, if there were anything in thy pocket but tavern reckonings, memorandums of bawdy houses, and one poor pennyworth of sugar candy to make thee long-winded —if thy pocket were enriched with any other injuries but these, I am a villain. And yet you will stand to it; you will not pocket up wrong? Art thou not ashamed?
Falstaff.	Dost thou hear, Hal? Thou knowest in the state of innocency Adam fell, and what should poor Jack Falstaff do in the days of villainy? Thou seest I have more flesh than another man, and therefore more frailty. You confess then, you picked my pocket?
Prince.	It appears so by the story.
Falstaff.	Hostess, I forgive thee, go make ready breakfast, love thy husband, look to thy servants, cherish thy guests. Thou shalt find me tractable to any honest reason. Thou seest I am pacified still. Nay, prithee be gone.
	[*Exit Hostess*]
	Now, Hal, to the news at court. For the robbery, lad—how is that answered?
Prince.	O my sweet beef, I must still be good angel to thee. The money is paid back again.
Falstaff.	O, I do not like that paying back! 'Tis a double labor.
Prince.	I am good friends with my father, and may do anything.
Falstaff.	Rob me the exchequer the first thing thou doest, and do it with unwashed hands too.
Bardolph.	Do, my lord.
Prince.	I have procured thee, Jack, a charge of foot.

Falstaff. I would it had been of horse. Where shall I find one that can steal well? O for a fine thief of the age of two and twenty or thereabouts! I am heinously unprovided. Well, God be thanked for these rebels, they offend none but the virtuous: I laud them, I praise them.

Prince. Bardolph!

Bardolph. My lord?

Prince. Go bear this letter to Lord John of Lancaster,
To my brother John; this to my Lord of Westmoreland.

               [*Exit Bardolph*]

Go, Peto, to horse, to horse; for thou and I
Have thirty miles to ride yet ere dinner time.

               [*Exit Peto*]

Jack, meet me tomorrow in the Temple Hall
At two o'clock in the afternoon.
There shalt thou know thy charge, and there receive
Money and order for their furniture.
The land is burning, Percy stands on high,
And either we or they must lower lie.

               [*Exit*]

Falstaff. Rare words! Brave world!
Hostess, my breakfast, come:
O, I could wish this tavern were my drum!

               [*Exit*]

PART I ACT FOUR

[Enter Hotspur, Worcester, and Douglas]

Hotspur. Well said, my noble Scot. If speaking truth
In this fine age were not thought flattery,
Such attribution should the Douglas have
As not a soldier of this season's stamp
Should go so general current through the world.
By God, I cannot flatter, I do defy
The tongues of soothers! But a braver place
In my heart's love hath no man than yourself.
Nay, task me to my word; approve me, lord.

Douglas. Thou art the king of honor.
No man so potent breathes upon the ground
But I will beard him.

[Enter one with letters]

Hotspur.   Do so, and 'tis well.—
What letters hast thou there?—I can but thank you.

Messenger. These letters come from your father.

Hotspur. Letters from him? Why comes he not himself?

Messenger. He cannot come, my lord, he is grievous sick.

Hotspur. Zounds! How has he the leisure to be sick
In such a justling time? Who leads his power?
Under whose government come they along?

Messenger.	His letters bears his mind, not I, my lord.
Worcester.	I prithee tell me, doth he keep his bed?
Messenger.	He did, my lord, four days ere I set forth,
	And at the time of my departure thence
	He was much feared by his physicians.
Worcester.	I would the state of time had first been whole
	Ere he by sickness had been visited.
	His health was never better worth than now.
Hotspur.	Sick now? Droop now? This sickness doth infect
	The very lifeblood of our enterprise.
	'Tis catching hither, even to our camp.
	He writes me here that inward sickness—
	And that his friends by deputation
	Could not so soon be drawn; nor did he think it meet
	To lay so dangerous and dear a trust
	On any soul removed but on his own.
	Yet doth he give us bold advertisement,
	That with our small conjunction we should on,
	To see how fortune is disposed to us;
	For, as he writes, there is no quailing now,
	Because the King is certainly possessed
	Of all our purposes. What say you to it?

Worcester.	Your father's sickness is a maim to us.
Hotspur.	A perilous gash, a very limb lopped off.
	And yet, in faith, it is not! His present want
	Seems more than we shall find it. Were it good
	To set the exact wealth of all our states
	All at one cast? To set so rich a main
	On the nice hazard of one doubtful hour?
	It were not good; for therein should we read
	The very bottom and the soul of hope,
	The very list, the very utmost bound
	Of all our fortunes.
Douglas.	Faith, and so we should.
	Where now remains a sweet reversion,
	We may boldly spend upon the hope of what is to come in.
	A comfort of retirement lives in this.
Hotspur.	A rendezvous, a home to fly unto,
	If that the devil and mischance look big
	Upon the maidenhead of our affairs.
Worcester.	But yet I would your father had been here.
	The quality and hair of our attempt
	Brooks no division. It will be thought
	By some that know not why he is away,
	That wisdom, loyalty, and mere dislike
	Of our proceedings kept the Earl from hence.
	And think how such an apprehension
	May turn the tide of fearful faction
	And breed a kind of question in our cause.

For well you know we of the off'ring side
Must keep aloof from strict arbitrament,
And stop all sight-holes, every loop from whence
The eye of reason may pry in upon us.
This absence of your father's draws a curtain
That shows the ignorant a kind of fear
Before not dreamt of.

Hotspur.   You strain too far.
I rather of his absence make this use:
It lends a luster and more great opinion,
A larger dare to our great enterprise,
Than if the Earl were here; for men must think,
If we, without his help, can make a head
To push against a kingdom, with his help
We shall o'erturn it topsy-turvy down.
Yet all goes well; yet all our joints are whole.

Douglas. As heart can think. There is not such a word
Spoke of in Scotland as this term of fear.

          [*Enter Sir Richard Vernon*]

Hotspur. My cousin Vernon, welcome, by my soul.

Vernon. Pray God my news be worth a welcome, lord.
The Earl of Westmoreland, seven thousand strong,
Is marching hitherwards; with him Prince John.

Hotspur. No harm. What more?

Vernon.   And further, I have learned
                    The King himself in person is set forth,
                    Or hitherwards intended speedily,
                    With strong and mighty preparation.

Hotspur.   He shall be welcome too. Where is his son,
                    The nimble-footed madcap Prince of Wales,
                    And his comrades, that daffed the world aside
                    And bid it pass?

Vernon.   All furnished, all in arms;
                    All plumed like estridges that with the wind
                    Bated like eagles having lately bathed;
                    Glittering in golden coats like images;
                    As full of spirit as the month of May
                    And gorgeous as the sun at midsummer;
                    Wanton as youthful goats, wild as young bulls.
                    I saw young Harry with his beaver on,
                    His cushes on his thighs, gallantly armed,
                    Rise from the ground like feathered Mercury,
                    And vaulted with such ease into his seat
                    As if an angel dropped down from the clouds
                    To turn and wind a fiery Pegasus
                    And witch the world with noble horsemanship.

Hotspur.	No more, no more! Worse than the sun in March,
	This praise doth nourish agues. Let them come.
	They come like sacrifices in their trim,
	And to the fire-eyed maid of smoky war
	All hot and bleeding will we offer them.
	The mailed Mars shall on his altars sit
	Up to the ears in blood. I am on fire
	To hear this rich reprisal is so nigh,
	And yet not ours. Come, let me taste my horse,
	Who is to bear me like a thunderbolt
	Against the bosom of the Prince of Wales.
	Harry to Harry shall, hot horse to horse,
	Meet, and ne'er part till one drop down a corse.
	O that Glendower were come!
Vernon.	There is more news.
	I learned in Worcester, as I rode along,
	He cannot draw his power this fourteen days.
Douglas.	That's the worst tidings that I hear of yet.
Worcester.	Ay, by my faith, that bears a frosty sound.
Hotspur.	What may the King's whole battle reach unto?
Vernon.	To thirty thousand.
Hotspur.	Forty let it be.
	My father and Glendower being both away,
	The powers of us may serve so great a day.
	Come, let us take a muster speedily.
	Doomsday is near. Die all, die merrily.
Douglas.	Talk not of dying. I am out of fear
	Of death or death's hand for this one half year. [*Exeunt*]

[Enter Falstaff and Bardolph]

Falstaff. Bardolph, get thee before to Coventry; fill me a bottle of sack. Our soldiers shall march through. We'll to Sutton Co'fil' tonight.

Bardolph. Will you give me money, captain?

Falstaff. Lay out, lay out.

Bardolph. This bottle makes an angel.

Falstaff. And if it do, take it for thy labor; and if it make twenty, take them all; I'll answer the coinage. Bid my lieutenant Peto meet me at town's end.

Bardolph. I will, captain. Farewell. *[Exit]*

Falstaff. If I be not ashamed of my soldiers, I am a soused gurnet. I have misused the King's press damnably. I have got, in exchange of a hundred and fifty soldiers, three hundred and odd pounds. I press me none but good householders, yeomen's sons; inquire me out contracted bachelors, such as had been asked twice on the banes—such a commodity of warm slaves as had as lief hear the devil as a drum, such as fear the report of a caliver worse than a struck fowl or a hurt wild duck. I pressed me none but such toasts-and-butter, with hearts in their bellies no bigger than pins' heads, and they have bought out their services; and now my whole charge consists of ancients, corporals, lieutenants, gentlemen of companies— slaves as ragged as Lazarus in the painted cloth, where the glutton's dogs licked his sores; and such as indeed were never soldiers, but discarded unjust serving-men, younger sons to younger brothers, revolted tapsters, and ostlers trade-fall'n; the cankers of a calm world and a long peace; ten times more dishonorable ragged than an old fazed ancient; and such have I to fill up the rooms of them as have bought out their services that you would think that I had a hundred and fifty tattered prodigals lately come from swine-keeping, from eating draff and husks. A mad fellow met me on the way, and told me I had unloaded all the gibbets and pressed the dead bodies. No eye hath seen such scarecrows.

I'll not march through Coventry with them, that's flat. Nay, and the villains march wide betwixt the legs, as if they had gyves on, for indeed I had the most of them out of prison. There's not a shirt and a half in all my company, and the half-shirt is two napkins tacked together and thrown over the shoulders like a herald's coat without sleeves; and the shirt, to say the truth, stol'n from my host at Saint Albans, or the red-nose innkeeper of Daventry. But that's all one; they'll find linen enough on every hedge.

[Enter the Prince and Westmoreland]

Prince. How now, blown Jack? How now, quilt?

Falstaff. What, Hal? How now, mad wag? What a devil dost thou in Warwickshire? My good Lord of Westmoreland, I cry you mercy. I thought your honor had already been at Shrewsbury.

Westmoreland. Faith, Sir John, 'tis more than time that I were there, and you too, but my powers are there already. The King, I can tell you, looks for us all, we must away all night.

Falstaff. Tut, never fear me: I am as vigilant as a cat to steal cream.

Prince. I think, to steal cream indeed, for thy theft hath already made thee butter. But tell me, Jack, whose fellows are these that come after?

Falstaff. Mine, Hal, mine.

Prince. I did never see such pitiful rascals.

Falstaff. Tut, tut, good enough to toss; food for powder, food for powder, they'll fill a pit as well as better. Tush, man, mortal men, mortal men.

Westmoreland. Ay, but, Sir John, methinks they are exceeding poor and bare, too beggarly.

Falstaff. Faith, for their poverty, I know not where they had that, and for their bareness, I am sure they never learned that of me.

Prince. No, I'll be sworn, unless you call three fingers in the ribs bare. But, sirrah, make haste. Percy is already in the field. [Exit]

Falstaff. What, is the King encamped?

Westmoreland. He is, Sir John. I fear we shall stay too long.

Falstaff. Well, to the latter end of a fray and the beginning of a feast fits a dull fighter and a keen guest.

[Exeunt]

[*Enter Hotspur, Worcester, Douglas, Vernon*]

Hotspur.	We'll fight with him tonight.
Worcester.	It may not be.
Douglas.	You give him then advantage.
Vernon.	Not a whit.
Hotspur.	Why say you so? Looks he not for supply?
Vernon.	So do we.
Hotspur.	His is certain, ours is doubtful.
Worcester.	Good cousin, be advised; stir not tonight.
Vernon.	Do not, my lord.
Douglas.	You do not counsel well.

You speak it out of fear and cold heart.

Vernon. Do me no slander, Douglas. By my life —
And I dare well maintain it with my life —
If well-respected honor bid me on,
I hold as little counsel with weak fear
As you, my lord, or any Scot that this day lives.
Let it be seen tomorrow in the battle
Which of us fears.

Douglas.	Yea, or tonight.
Vernon.	Content.
Hotspur.	Tonight, say I.

Vernon. Come, come, it may not be.
I wonder much, being men of such great leading as you are,
That you foresee not what impediments
Drag back our expedition. Certain horse
Of my cousin Vernon's are not yet come up.
Your uncle Worcester's horse came but today;
And now their pride and mettle is asleep,
Their courage with hard labor tame and dull,
That not a horse is half the half of himself.

Hotspur. So are the horses of the enemy
In general journey-bated and brought low.
The better part of ours are full of rest.

Worcester. The number of the King exceedeth ours.
For God's sake, cousin, stay till all come in.

[The trumpet sounds a parley.
Then Sir Walter Blunt enters]

Blunt. I come with gracious offers from the King,
If you vouchsafe me hearing and respect.

Hotspur. Welcome, Sir Walter Blunt, and would to God
You were of our determination.
Some of us love you well; and even those some
Envy your great deservings and good name,
Because you are not of our quality,
But stand against us like an enemy.

Blunt. And God defend but still I should stand so,
So long as out of limit and true rule
You stand against anointed majesty.
But to my charge. The King hath sent to know
The nature of your griefs, and whereupon
You conjure from the breast of civil peace
Such bold hostility, teaching his duteous land
Audacious cruelty. If that the King
Have any way your good deserts forgot,
Which he confesseth to be manifold,
He bids you name your griefs, and with all speed
You shall have your desires with interest,
And pardon absolute for yourself and these
Herein misled by your suggestion.

Hotspur. The King is kind, and well we know the King
Knows at what time to promise, when to pay.
My father and my uncle and myself
Did give him that same royalty he wears;
And when he was not six and twenty strong,
Sick in the world's regard, wretched and low,
A poor unminded outlaw sneaking home,
My father gave him welcome to the shore;
And when he heard him swear and vow to God
He came but to be Duke of Lancaster,
To sue his livery and beg his peace,
With tears of innocency and terms of zeal,
My father, in kind heart and pity moved,

Swore him assistance, and performed it too.
Now when the lords and barons of the realm
Perceived Northumberland did lean to him,
The more and less came in with cap and knee;
Met him in boroughs, cities, villages,
Attended him on bridges, stood in lanes,
Laid gifts before him, proffered him their oaths,
Gave him their heirs as pages, followed him
Even at the heels in golden multitudes.
He presently, as greatness knows itself,
Steps me a little higher than his vow
Made to my father, while his blood was poor,
Upon the naked shore at Ravenspurgh;
And now, forsooth, takes on him to reform
Some certain edicts and some strait decrees
That lie too heavy on the commonwealth;
Cries out upon abuses, seems to weep
Over his country's wrongs; and by this face,
This seeming brow of justice, did he win
The hearts of all that he did angle for;
Proceeded further—cut me off the heads
Of all the favorites that the absent king
In deputation left behind him here
When he was personal in the Irish war.

Blunt.   Tut! I came not to hear this.

Hotspur.   Then to the point.
In short time after, he deposed the King;
Soon after that deprived him of his life;
And in the neck of that tasked the whole state;
To make that worse, suff'red his kinsman March
(Who is, if every owner were well placed,
Indeed his king) to be engaged in Wales,
There without ransom to lie forfeited;
Disgraced me in my happy victories,
Sought to entrap me by intelligence;
Rated mine uncle from the council board;
In rage dismissed my father from the court;
Broke oath on oath, committed wrong on wrong;
And in conclusion drove us to seek out
This head of safety, and withal to pry
Into his title, the which we find
Too indirect for long continuance.

Blunt. Shall I return this answer to the King?

Hotspur. No so, Sir Walter. We'll withdraw awhile.
Go to the King; and let there be impawned
Some surety for a safe return again,
And in the morning early shall mine uncle
Bring him our purposes; and so farewell.

Blunt. I would you would accept of grace and love.

Hotspur. And may be so we shall.

Blunt. Pray God you do.

            [*Exeunt*]

[Enter the Archbishop of York and Sir Michael]

Archbishop. Hie, good Sir Michael; bear this sealed brief
With winged haste to the Lord Marshal;
This to my cousin Scroop; and all the rest
To whom they are directed. If you knew
How much they do import, you would make haste.

Sir Michael. My good lord, I guess their tenor.

Archbishop. Like enough you do.
Tomorrow, good Sir Michael, is a day
Wherein the fortune of ten thousand men
Must bide the touch; for, sir, at Shrewsbury,
As I am truly given to understand,
The King with mighty and quick-raised power
Meets with Lord Harry; and I fear, Sir Michael,
What with the sickness of Northumberland,
Whose power was in the first proportion,
And what with Owen Glendower's absence thence,
Who with them was a rated sinew too
And comes not in, overruled by prophecies —
I fear the power of Percy is too weak
To wage an instant trial with the King.

Sir Michael. Why, my good lord, you need not fear;
There is Douglas and Lord Mortimer.

Archbishop.	No, Mortimer is not there.
Sir Michael.	But there is Mordake, Vernon, Lord Harry Percy,
	And there is my Lord of Worcester, and a head
	Of gallant warriors, noble gentlemen.
Archbishop.	And so there is; but yet the King hath drawn
	The special head of all the land together—
	The Prince of Wales, Lord John of Lancaster,
	The noble Westmoreland and warlike Blunt,
	And many more corrivals and dear men
	Of estimation and command in arms.
Sir Michael.	Doubt not, my lord, they shall be well opposed.
Archbishop.	I hope no less, yet needful 'tis to fear;
	And, to prevent the worst, Sir Michael, speed.
	For if Lord Percy thrive not, ere the King
	Dismiss his power, he means to visit us,
	For he hath heard of our confederacy,
	And 'tis but wisdom to make strong against him.
	Therefore make haste. I must go write again
	To other friends; and so farewell, Sir Michael.

       [Exeunt]

PART I ACT FIVE

[*Enter the King, Prince of Wales, Lord John of Lancaster,
the Earl of Westmoreland, Sir Walter Blunt, and Falstaff*]

King.   How bloodily the sun begins to peer
    Above yon bulky hill! The day looks pale
    At his distemp'rature.

Prince.   The southern wind
    Doth play the trumpet to his purposes
    And by his hollow whistling in the leaves
    Foretells a tempest and a blust'ring day.

King.   Then with the losers let it sympathize,
    For nothing can seem foul to those that win.

          [*Trumpets. Enter Worcester and Vernon*]

    How now, my Lord of Worcester? 'Tis not well
    That you and I should meet upon such terms
    As now we meet. You have deceived our trust
    And made us doff our easy robes of peace
    To crush our old limbs in ungentle steel.
    This is not well, my lord; this is not well.
    What say you to it? Will you again unknit
    This churlish knot of all-abhorred war,
    And move in that obedient orb again
    Where you did give a fair and natural light,
    And be no more an exhaled meteor,
    A prodigy of fear, and a portent
    Of broached mischief to the unborn times?

Worcester.	Hear me, my liege.
	For mine own part, I could be well content
	To entertain the lag-end of my life
	With quiet hours, for I protest
	I have not sought the day of this dislike.
King.	You have not sought it! How comes it then?
Falstaff.	Rebellion lay in his way, and he found it.
Prince.	Peace, chewet, peace!
Worcester.	It pleased your Majesty to turn your looks
	Of favor from myself and all our house;
	And yet I must remember you, my lord,
	We were the first and dearest of your friends.
	For you my staff of office did I break
	In Richard's time, and posted day and night
	To meet you on the way and kiss your hand
	When yet you were in place and in account
	Nothing so strong and fortunate as I.
	It was myself, my brother, and his son
	That brought you home and boldly did outdare
	The dangers of the time. You swore to us,
	And you did swear that oath at Doncaster,
	That you did nothing purpose 'gainst the state,
	Nor claim no further than your new-fall'n right,
	The seat of Gaunt, dukedom of Lancaster.
	To this we swore our aid. But in short space
	It rained down fortune show'ring on your head,

And such a flood of greatness fell on you —
What with our help, what with the absent King,
What with the injuries of a wanton time,
The seeming sufferances that you had borne,
And the contrarious winds that held the King
So long in his unlucky Irish wars
That all in England did repute him dead —
And from this swarm of fair advantages
You took occasion to be quickly wooed
To gripe the general sway into your hand;
Forgot your oath to us at Doncaster;
And, being fed by us, you used us so
As that ungentle gull, the cuckoo's bird,
Useth the sparrow—did oppress our nest,
Grew by our feeding to so great a bulk
That even our love durst not come near your sight
For fear of swallowing; but with nimble wing
We were enforced for safety sake to fly
Out of your sight and raise this present head;
Whereby we stand opposed by such means
As you yourself have forged against yourself
By unkind usage, dangerous countenance,
And violation of all faith and troth
Sworn to us in your younger enterprise.

King.	These things, indeed, you have articulate,
	Proclaimed at market crosses, read in churches,
	To face the garment of rebellion
	With some fine color that may please the eye
	Of fickle changelings and poor discontents,
	Which gape and rub the elbow at the news
	Of hurlyburly innovation.
	And never yet did insurrection want
	Such water colors to impaint his cause,
	Nor moody beggars, starving for a time
	Of pell-mell havoc and confusion.
Prince.	In both your armies there is many a soul
	Shall pay full dearly for this encounter,
	If once they join in trial. Tell your nephew
	The Prince of Wales doth join with all the world
	In praise of Henry Percy. By my hopes,
	This present enterprise set off his head,
	I do not think a braver gentleman,
	More active-valiant or more valiant-young,
	More daring or more bold, is now alive
	To grace this latter age with noble deeds.
	For my part, I may speak it to my shame,
	I have a truant been to chivalry;
	And so I hear he doth account me too.
	Yet this before my father's majesty—
	I am content that he shall take the odds
	Of his great name and estimation,
	And will, to save the blood on either side,
	Try fortune with him in a single fight.

King.	And, Prince of Wales, so dare we venture thee;
	Albeit, considerations infinite
	Do make against it. No, good Worcester, no!
	We love our people well; even those we love
	That are misled upon your cousin's part;
	And, will they take the offer of our grace,
	Both he, and they, and you, yea, every man
	Shall be my friend again, and I'll be his.
	So tell your cousin, and bring me word
	What he will do. But if he will not yield,
	Rebuke and dread correction wait on us,
	And they shall do their office. So be gone.
	We will not now be troubled with reply.
	We offer fair; take it advisedly.

[Exit Worcester with Vernon]

Prince.	It will not be accepted, on my life.
	The Douglas and the Hotspur both together
	Are confident against the world in arms.
King.	Hence, therefore, every leader to his charge;
	For, on their answer, will we set on them,
	And God befriend us as our cause is just!

[Exeunt. Manent Prince and Falstaff]

Falstaff.	Hal, if thou see me down in the battle and bestride me, so! 'Tis a point of friendship.
Prince.	Nothing but a colossus can do thee that friendship. Say thy prayers, and farewell.
Falstaff.	I would 'twere bedtime, Hal, and all well.
Prince.	Why, thou owest God a death.
	[*Exit*]
Falstaff.	'Tis not due yet: I would be loath to pay him before his day. What need I be so forward with him that calls not on me? Well, 'tis no matter; honor pricks me on. Yea, but how if honor prick me off when I come on? How then? Can honor set to a leg? No. Or an arm? No. Or take away the grief of a wound? No. Honor hath no skill in surgery then? No. What is honor? A word. What is in that word honor? What is that honor? Air—a trim reckoning! Who hath it? He that died a Wednesday. Doth he feel it? No. Doth he hear it? No. 'Tis insensible then? Yea, to the dead. But will it not live with the living? No. Why? Detraction will not suffer it. Therefore I'll none of it. Honor is a mere scutcheon—and so ends my catechism.
	[*Exit*]

[*Enter Worcester and Sir Richard Vernon*]

Worcester.   O no, my nephew must not know, Sir Richard,

The liberal and kind offer of the King.

Vernon.   'Twere best he did.

Worcester.   Then are we all undone.

It is not possible, it cannot be,

The King should keep his word in loving us.

He will suspect us still and find a time

To punish this offense in other faults.

Supposition all our lives shall be stuck full of eyes;

For treason is but trusted like the fox,

Who, never so tame, so cherished and locked up,

Will have a wild trick of his ancestors.

Look how we can, or sad or merrily,

Interpretation will misquote our looks,

And we shall feed like oxen at a stall,

The better cherished still the nearer death.

My nephew's trespass may be well forgot;

It hath the excuse of youth and heat of blood,

And an adopted name of privilege —

A hare-brained Hotspur, governed by a spleen.

All his offenses live upon my head

And on his father's. We did train him on;

And, his corruption being ta'en from us,
We, as the spring of all, shall pay for all.
Therefore, good cousin, let not Harry know,
In any case, the offer of the King.

Vernon. Deliver what you will, I'll say 'tis so.
Here comes your cousin.

[*Enter Hotspur and Douglas*]

Hotspur.   My uncle is returned.
Deliver up my Lord of Westmoreland.
Uncle, what news?

Worcester. The King will bid you battle presently.

Douglas. Defy him by the Lord of Westmoreland.

Hotspur. Lord Douglas, go you and tell him so.

Douglas. Marry, and shall, and very willingly.

[*Exit*]

Worcester. There is no seeming mercy in the King.

Hotspur. Did you beg any? God forbid!

Worcester. I told him gently of our grievances,
Of his oath-breaking, which he mended thus,
By now forswearing that he is forsworn.
He calls us rebels, traitors, and will scourge
With haughty arms this hateful name in us.

[*Enter Douglas*]

Douglas. Arm, gentlemen, to arms, for I have thrown
A brave defiance in King Henry's teeth,
And Westmoreland, that was engaged, did bear it;
Which cannot choose but bring him quickly on.

Worcester.	The Prince of Wales stepped forth before the King
	And, nephew, challenged you to single fight.
Hotspur.	O, would the quarrel lay upon our heads,
	And that no man might draw short breath today
	But I and Harry Monmouth! Tell me, tell me,
	How showed his tasking? Seemed it in contempt?
Vernon.	No, by my soul. I never in my life
	Did hear a challenge urged more modestly,
	Unless a brother should a brother dare
	To gentle exercise and proof of arms.
	He gave you all the duties of a man;
	Trimmed up your praises with a princely tongue;
	Spoke your deservings like a chronicle;
	Making you ever better than his praise
	By still dispraising praise valued with you;
	And, which became him like a prince indeed,
	He made a blushing cital of himself,
	And chid his truant youth with such a grace
	As if he mast'red there a double spirit
	Of teaching and of learning instantly.
	There did he pause; but let me tell the world,
	If he outlive the envy of this day,
	England did never owe so sweet a hope,
	So much misconstrued in his wantonness.

Hotspur. Cousin, I think thou art enamored
On his follies. Never did I hear
Of any prince so wild a liberty.
But be he as he will, yet once ere night
I will embrace him with a soldier's arm,
That he shall shrink under my courtesy.
Arm, arm with speed! And, fellows, soldiers, friends,
Better consider what you have to do
Than I, that have not well the gift of tongue,
Can lift your blood up with persuasion.

       [Enter a Messenger]

Messenger. My lord, here are letters for you.
Hotspur. I cannot read them now.—
O gentlemen, the time of life is short!
To spend that shortness basely were too long
If life did ride upon a dial's point,
Still ending at the arrival of an hour.
And if we live, we live to tread on kings;
If die, brave death, when princes die with us!
Now for our consciences, the arms are fair,
When the intent of bearing them is just.

[Enter another Messenger]

Messenger. My lord, prepare. The King comes on apace.

Hotspur. I thank him that he cuts me from my tale,
For I profess not talking: only this —
Let each man do his best; and here draw I
A sword whose temper I intend to stain
With the best blood that I can meet withal
In the adventure of this perilous day.
Now, Esperance! Percy! and set on.
Sound all the lofty instruments of war,
And by that music let us all embrace;
For, heaven to earth, some of us never shall
A second time do such a courtesy.

[They embrace, the trumpets sound, the
King enters with his power. Alarum to the
battle. Exeunt. Then enter Douglas, and
Sir Walter Blunt disguised as the King]

Blunt. What is thy name, that in battle thus thou crossest me?
What honor dost thou seek upon my head?

Douglas. Know then my name is Douglas,
And I do haunt thee in the battle thus
Because some tell me that thou art a king.

Blunt. They tell thee true.

Douglas. The Lord of Stafford dear today hath bought
Thy likeness, for instead of thee, King Harry,
This sword hath ended him: so shall it thee,
Unless thou yield thee as my prisoner.

Blunt. I was not born a yielder, thou proud Scot;
And thou shalt find a king that will revenge
Lord Stafford's death.

        [They fight. Blunt is slain by
        Douglas. Then enter Hotspur]

Hotspur. O Douglas, hadst thou fought at Holmedon thus,
I never had triumphed upon a Scot.

Douglas. All's done, all's won: here breathless lies the King.

Hotspur. Where?

Douglas. Here.

Hotspur. This, Douglas? No. I know this face full well.
A gallant knight he was, his name was Blunt;
Semblably furnished like the King himself.

Douglas. A fool go with thy soul, whither it goes!
A borrowed title hast thou bought too dear:
Why didst thou tell me that thou wert a king?

Hotspur. The King hath many marching in his coats.

Douglas. Now, by my sword, I will kill all his coats;
I'll murder all his wardrobe, piece by piece,
Until I meet the King.

Hotspur.   Up and away!
Our soldiers stand full fairly for the day.

        [Exeunt]

[Alarum. Enter Falstaff solus]

Falstaff.   Though I could scape shot-free at London, I fear the shot here. Here's no scoring but upon the pate. Soft! Who are you? Sir Walter Blunt. There's honor for you! Here's no vanity! I am as hot as molten lead, and as heavy too. God keep lead out of me. I need no more weight than mine own bowels. I have led my rag-of-muffins where they are peppered. There's not three of my hundred and fifty left alive, and they are for the town's end, to beg during life. But who comes here?

[Enter the Prince]

Prince.   What, stands thou idle here? Lend me thy sword.
                        Many a nobleman lies stark and stiff
                        Under the hoofs of vaunting enemies,
                        Whose deaths are yet unrevenged.
                        I prithee lend me thy sword.

Falstaff.   O Hal, I prithee give me leave to breathe awhile. Turk Gregory never did such deeds in arms as I have done this day. I have paid Percy, I have made him sure.

Prince.   He is indeed, and living to kill thee.
                        I prithee lend me thy sword.

Falstaff.   Nay, before God, Hal, if Percy be alive, thou gets not my sword; but take my pistol if thou wilt.

Prince.   Give it me. What, is it in the case?

Falstaff.   Ay, Hal. 'Tis hot, 'tis hot. There's that will sack a city.

[The Prince draws out a bottle of sack]

Prince.   What, is it a time to jest and dally now?

[He throws the bottle at him. Exit]

Falstaff.   Well, if Percy be alive, I'll pierce him. If he do come in my way, so; if he do not, if I come in his willingly, let him make a carbonado of me. I like not such grinning honor as Sir Walter hath. Give me life; which if I can save, so; if not, honor comes unlooked for, and there's an end. *[Exit]*

[Alarum. Excursions. Enter the King, the Prince,
Lord John of Lancaster, Earl of Westmoreland]

King.   I prithee, Harry, withdraw thyself, thou bleedest too much.
    Lord John of Lancaster, go you with him.

John.   Not I, my lord, unless I did bleed too.

Prince.   I beseech your Majesty make up,
    Lest your retirement do amaze your friends.

King.   I will do so. My Lord of Westmoreland, lead him to his tent.

Westmoreland.   Come, my lord, I'll lead you to your tent.

Prince.   Lead me, my lord? I do not need your help;
    And God forbid a shallow scratch should drive
    The Prince of Wales from such a field as this,
    Where stained nobility lies trodden on,
    And rebels' arms triumph in massacres!

John.   We breathe too long. Come, cousin Westmoreland,
    Our duty this way lies. For God's sake, come.

[Exeunt Lancaster and Westmoreland]

Prince.   By heaven, thou hast deceived me, Lancaster!
    I did not think thee lord of such a spirit.
    Before, I loved thee as a brother, John,
    But now I do respect thee as my soul.

King.   I saw him hold Lord Percy at the point
    With lustier maintenance than I did look for
    Of such an ungrown warrior.

Prince.   O, this boy lends mettle to us all! *[Exit]*

Douglas. Another king? They grow like Hydra's heads.
I am the Douglas, fatal to all those
That wear those colors on them. What art thou
That counterfeit'st the person of a king?

King. The King himself, who, Douglas, grieves at heart
So many of his shadows thou hast met,
And not the very King. I have two boys
Seek Percy and thyself about the field;
But, seeing thou fall'st on me so luckily,
I will assay thee, and defend thyself.

Douglas. I fear thou art another counterfeit;
And yet, in faith, thou bearest thee like a king.
But mine I am sure thou art, whoe'er thou be,
And thus I win thee.

*[They fight, the King being in
danger. Enter Prince of Wales]*

Prince. Hold up thy head, vile Scot, or thou art like
Never to hold it up again. The spirits
Of valiant Shirley, Stafford, Blunt are in my arms.
It is the Prince of Wales that threatens thee,
Who never promiseth but he means to pay.

[They fight. Douglas flees]

Cheerly, my lord. How fares your Grace?
Sir Nicholas Gawsey hath for succor sent,
And so hath Clifton. I'll to Clifton straight.

King.   Stay and breathe awhile.
Thou hast redeemed thy lost opinion,
And showed thou mak'st some tender of my life,
In this fair rescue thou hast brought to me.

Prince.   O God, they did me too much injury
That ever said I heark'ned for your death.
If it were so, I might have let alone
The insulting hand of Douglas over you,
Which would have been as speedy in your end
As all the poisonous potions in the world,
And saved the treacherous labor of your son.

King.   Make up to Clifton; I'll to Sir Nicholas Gawsey.

        [*Exit. Enter Hotspur*]

Hotspur.   If I mistake not, thou art Harry Monmouth.

Prince.   Thou speak'st as if I would deny my name.

Hotspur.   My name is Harry Percy.

Prince.   Why, then I see a very valiant rebel of the name.
I am the Prince of Wales, and think not, Percy,
To share with me in glory any more.
Two stars keep not their motion in one sphere,
Nor can one England brook a double reign
Of Harry Percy and the Prince of Wales.

Hotspur.   Nor shall it, Harry, for the hour is come
To end the one of us; and would to God
Thy name in arms were now as great as mine!

Prince.	I'll make it greater ere I part from thee,
	And all the budding honors on thy crest
	I'll crop to make a garland for my head.
Hotspur.	I can no longer brook thy vanities.

[They fight. Enter Falstaff]

Falstaff.	Well said, Hal! To it, Hal!
	Nay, you shall find no boy's play here,
	I can tell you.

*[Enter Douglas. He fights with Falstaff
who falls down as if he were dead.
Exit Douglas. The Prince kills Percy]*

Hotspur.	O Harry, thou hast robbed me of my youth!
	I better brook the loss of brittle life
	Than those proud titles thou hast won of me.
	They wound my thoughts worse than thy sword my flesh.
	But thoughts, the slaves of life, and life, time's fool,
	And time, that takes survey of all the world,
	Must have a stop. O, I could prophesy,
	But that the earthy and cold hand of death
	Lies on my tongue. No, Percy, thou art dust,
	And food for — *[Dies]*

Prince.   For worms, brave Percy. Fare thee well, great heart.
          Ill-weaved ambition, how much art thou shrunk!
          When that this body did contain a spirit,
          A kingdom for it was too small a bound;
          But now two paces of the vilest earth
          Is room enough. This earth that bears thee dead
          Bears not alive so stout a gentleman.
          If thou wert sensible of courtesy,
          I should not make so dear a show of zeal.
          But let my favors hide thy mangled face;
          And, even in thy behalf, I'll thank myself
          For doing these fair rites of tenderness.
          Adieu, and take thy praise with thee to heaven.
          Thy ignominy sleep with thee in the grave,
          But not rememb'red in thy epitaph.

               [*He spies Falstaff on the ground*]

          What, old acquaintance? Could not all this flesh
          Keep in a little life? Poor Jack, farewell!
          I could have better spared a better man.
          O, I should have a heavy miss of thee
          If I were much in love with vanity.
          Death hath not struck so fat a deer today,
          Though many dearer, in this bloody fray.
          Emboweled will I see thee by-and-by;
          Till then in blood by noble Percy lie.

               [*Exit*]

[Falstaff rises up]

Falstaff. Emboweled? If thou embowel me today, I'll give you leave to powder me and eat me too tomorrow. 'Sblood, 'twas time to counterfeit, or that hot termagant Scot had paid me scot and lot too. Counterfeit? I lie; I am no counterfeit. To die is to be a counterfeit, for he is but the counterfeit of a man who hath not the life of a man; but to counterfeit dying when a man thereby liveth, is to be no counterfeit, but the true and perfect image of life indeed. The better part of valor is discretion, in the which better part I have saved my life. Zounds, I am afraid of this gunpowder Percy, though he be dead. How if he should counterfeit too, and rise? By my faith, I am afraid he would prove the better counterfeit. Therefore I'll make him sure; yea, and I'll swear I killed him. Why may not he rise as well as I? Nothing confutes me but eyes, and nobody sees me. Therefore, sirrah [stabs him], with a new wound in your thigh, come you along with me.

[He takes up Hotspur upon his back.
Enter Prince and John of Lancaster]

Prince. Come, brother John; full bravely hast thou fleshed
Thy maiden sword.

John. But, soft! whom have we here?
Did you not tell me this fat man was dead?

Prince. I did; I saw him dead,
Breathless and bleeding on the ground. Art thou alive,
Or is it fantasy that plays upon our eyesight?
I prithee speak. We will not trust our eyes
Without our ears. Thou art not what thou seem'st.

Falstaff. No, that's certain, I am not a double man; but if I be not Jack Falstaff, then am I a Jack. There is Percy. If your father will do me any honor, so; if not, let him kill the next Percy himself. I look to be either earl or duke, I can assure you.

Prince. Why, Percy I killed myself, and saw thee dead!

Falstaff. Didst thou? Lord, Lord, how this world is given to lying. I grant you I was down, and out of breath, and so was he; but we rose both at an instant and fought a long hour by Shrewsbury clock. If I may be believed, so; if not, let them that should reward valor bear the sin upon their own heads. I'll take it upon my death, I gave him this wound in the thigh. If the man were alive and would deny it, zounds! I would make him eat a piece of my sword.

John. This is the strangest tale that ever I heard.

Prince. This is the strangest fellow, brother John.
Come, bring your luggage nobly on your back.
For my part, if a lie may do thee grace,
I'll gild it with the happiest terms I have.

[*A retreat is sounded*]

The trumpet sounds retreat; the day is ours.
Come, brother, let us to the highest of the field,
To see what friends are living, who are dead.

[*Exeunt Prince Henry and Prince John*]

Falstaff. I'll follow, as they say, for reward. He that rewards me, God reward him. If I do grow great, I'll grow less; for I'll purge, and leave sack, and live cleanly, as a nobleman should do.

[*Exit, bearing off the body*]

[*Trumpets sound. Enter the King, the Prince of Wales, Lord John of Lancaster, the Earl of West-moreland, with Worcester and Vernon prisoners*]

King. Thus ever did rebellion find rebuke.

Ill-spirited Worcester, did not we send grace,

Pardon, and terms of love to all of you?

And wouldst thou turn our offers contrary?

Misuse the tenor of thy kinsman's trust?

Three knights upon our party slain today,

A noble earl, and many a creature else

Had been alive this hour,

If like a Christian thou hadst truly borne

Betwixt our armies true intelligence.

Worcester. What I have done my safety urged me to;

And I embrace this fortune patiently,

Since not to be avoided it falls on me.

King. Bear Worcester to the death, and Vernon too;

Other offenders we will pause upon.

[*Exeunt Worcester and Vernon, guarded*]

How goes the field?

Prince.	The noble Scot, Lord Douglas, when he saw
	The fortune of the day quite turned from him,
	The noble Percy slain, and all his men
	Upon the foot of fear, fled with the rest;
	And falling from a hill, he was so bruised
	That the pursuers took him. At my tent
	The Douglas is, and I beseech your Grace
	I may dispose of him.
King.	With all my heart.
Prince.	Then, brother John of Lancaster, to you
	This honorable bounty shall belong.
	Go to the Douglas and deliver him
	Up to his pleasure, ransomless and free.
	His valors shown upon our crests today
	Have taught us how to cherish such high deeds,
	Even in the bosom of our adversaries.
John.	I thank your Grace for this high courtesy,
	Which I shall give away immediately.
King.	Then this remains, that we divide our power.
	You, son John, and my cousin Westmoreland,
	Towards York shall bend you with your dearest speed
	To meet Northumberland and the prelate Scroop,

Who, as we hear, are busily in arms.
Myself and you, son Harry, will towards Wales
To fight with Glendower and the Earl of March.
Rebellion in this land shall lose his sway,
Meeting the check of such another day;
And since this business so fair is done,
Let us not leave till all our own be won. [*Exeunt*]

FINIS—PART ONE

SCENE

England: London and parts of the country. Circa 1400.

DRAMATIS PERSONAE — Part II

RUMOR, *the Presenter*
HENRY IV, *King of England*
PRINCE HENRY, *afterwards crowned King Henry V*
PRINCE JOHN OF LANCASTER, *son to Henry IV*
GLOUCESTER, CLARENCE, *sons to Henry IV*
EARL OF WESTMORELAND, *with the King's Party*
EARLS OF WARWICK, SURREY, *with the King's Party*
LORD CHIEF JUSTICE, *with the King's Party*
GOWER, HARCOURT, *with the King's Party*
EARL OF NORTHUMBERLAND, *opponent of the King*
ARCHBISHOP OF YORK, *opponent of the King*
LORDS MOWBRAY, HASTINGS, BARDOLPH, *opponents of the King*
TRAVERS, MORTON, COLEVILLE, *opponents of the King*
SIR JOHN FALSTAFF, *irregular humorist*
POINS, PISTOL, *irregular humorists*
PETO, BARDOLPH, *irregular humorists*
SHALLOW, SILENCE, *country justices*
SHADOW, BULLCALF, *country soldiers*
MOLDY, WART, FEEBLE, *country soldiers*
FANG, SNARE, *sergeants*
LADY NORTHUMBERLAND, *wife to the Earl of Northumberland*
LADY PERCY, *widow of "Hotspur" (son of Northumberland)*
MISTRESS QUICKLY, *hostess of the tavern*
DOLL TEARSHEET, *of the tavern*
EPILOGUE, SOLDIERS, SERVANTS, BEADLES AND OTHERS

PART II ACT ONE

INTRODUCTION–SCENE I

[*Enter Rumor, painted full of tongues*]

Rumor. Open your ears, for which of you will stop
The vent of hearing when loud Rumor speaks?
I, from the orient to the drooping west,
Making the wind my post-horse, still unfold
The acts commenced on this ball of earth.
Upon my tongues continual slanders ride,
The which in every language I pronounce,
Stuffing the ears of men with false reports.
I speak of peace while covert enmity
Under the smile of safety wounds the world.
And who but Rumor, who but only I,
Make fearful musters and prepared defense
Whiles the big year, swoln with some other grief,
Is thought with child by the stern tyrant, war,
And no such matter? Rumor is a pipe
Blown by surmises, jealousies, conjectures,
And of so easy and so plain a stop
That the blunt monster with uncounted heads,
The still-discordant wav'ring multitude,
Can play upon it. But what need I thus
My well-known body to anatomize
Among my household? Why is Rumor here?

I run before King Harry's victory,
Who in a bloody field by Shrewsbury
Hath beaten down young Hotspur and his troops,
Quenching the flame of bold rebellion
Even with the rebels' blood. But what mean I
To speak so true at first? My office is
To noise abroad that Harry Monmouth fell
Under the wrath of noble Hotspur's sword,
And that the King before the Douglas' rage
Stooped his anointed head as low as death.
This have I rumored through the peasant towns
Between that royal field of Shrewsbury
And this worm-eaten hole of ragged stone,
Where Hotspur's father, old Northumberland,
Lies crafty-sick. The posts come tiring on,
And not a man of them brings other news
Than they have learned of me. From Rumor's tongues
They bring smooth comforts false, worse than true wrongs.

[*Exit Rumor*]

[Enter the Lord Bardolph and the Porter]

Lord Bardolph. Who keeps the gate here, ho? Where is the Earl?

Porter. *[Within]* What shall I say you are?

Lord Bardolph.   Tell thou the Earl
That the Lord Bardolph doth attend him here.

Porter. His lordship is walked forth into the orchard.
Please it your honor, knock but at the gate,
And he himself will answer.

[Enter the Earl of Northumberland]

Lord Bardolph.   Here comes the Earl.

Northumberland. What news, Lord Bardolph? Every minute now
Should be the father of some stratagem.
The times are wild. Contention, like a horse
Full of high feeding, madly hath broke loose
And bears down all before him.

Lord Bardolph.   Noble Earl,
I bring you certain news from Shrewsbury.

Northumberland. Good, and God will!

Lord Bardolph.   As good as heart can wish.
The King is almost wounded to the death;
And, in the fortune of my lord your son,
Prince Harry slain outright; and both the Blunts
Killed by the hand of Douglas; young Prince John
And Westmoreland and Stafford fled the field;
And Harry Monmouth's brawn, the hulk Sir John,

Is prisoner to your son. O, such a day,
So fought, so followed, and so fairly won,
Came not till now to dignify the times
Since Caesar's fortunes!

Northumberland. How is this derived?
Saw you the field? Came you from Shrewsbury?

Lord Bardolph. I spake with one, my lord, that came from thence,

[*Enter Travers*]

A gentleman well bred and of good name,
That freely rend'red me these news for true.

Northumberland. Here comes my servant Travers, who I sent
On Tuesday last to listen after news.

Lord Bardolph. My lord, I overrode him on the way,
And he is furnished with no certainties
More than he haply may retail from me.

Northumberland. Now, Travers, what good tidings comes with you?

Travers. My lord, Sir John Umfrevile turned me back
With joyful tidings, and, being better horsed,
Outrode me. After him came spurring hard
A gentleman, almost forspent with speed,
That stopped by me to breathe his bloodied horse.
He asked the way to Chester, and of him
I did demand what news from Shrewsbury.
He told me that rebellion had bad luck,
And that young Harry Percy's spur was cold.
With that, he gave his able horse the head,
And bending forward struck his armed heels

Against the panting sides of his poor jade
Up to the rowel-head, and starting so
He seemed in running to devour the way,
Staying no longer question.

Northumberland.   Ha? Again.
Said he young Harry Percy's spur was cold?
Of Hotspur Coldspur? That rebellion
Had met ill luck?

Lord Bardolph.   My lord, I'll tell you what.
If my young lord your son have not the day,
Upon mine honor, for a silken point
I'll give my barony. Never talk of it.

Northumberland. Why should that gentleman that rode by Travers
Give then such instances of loss?

Lord Bardolph.   Who, he?
He was some hilding fellow that had stol'n
The horse he rode on, and, upon my life,
Spoke at a venture. Look, here comes more news.

                    [*Enter Morton*]

Northumberland. Yea, this man's brow, like to a titleleaf,
Foretells the nature of a tragic volume.
So looks the strond whereon the imperious flood
Hath left a witnessed usurpation.
Say, Morton, didst thou come from Shrewsbury?

Morton. I ran from Shrewsbury, my noble lord,
Where hateful death put on his ugliest mask
To fright our party.

Northumberland.	How doth my son and brother?
	Thou tremblest, and the whiteness in thy cheek
	Is apter than thy tongue to tell thy errand.
	Even such a man, so faint, so spiritless,
	So dull, so dead in look, so woebegone,
	Drew Priam's curtain in the dead of night,
	And would have told him half his Troy was burnt.
	But Priam found the fire ere he his tongue
	And I my Percy's death ere thou report'st it.
	This thou wouldst say, "Your son did thus and thus;
	Your brother thus. So fought the noble Douglas,"
	Stopping my greedy ear with their bold deeds.
	But in the end, to stop my ear indeed,
	Thou hast a sigh to blow away this praise,
	Ending with "Brother, son, and all are dead."
Morton.	Douglas is living, and your brother—yet;
	But, for my lord your son—
Northumberland.	Why, he is dead!
	See what a ready tongue suspicion hath!
	He that but fears the thing he would not know
	Hath by instinct knowledge from others' eyes
	That what he feared is chanced. Yet speak, Morton.
	Tell thou an earl his divination lies,
	And I will take it as a sweet disgrace
	And make thee rich for doing me such wrong.
Morton.	You are too great to be by me gainsaid.
	Your spirit is too true, your fears too certain.

Northumberland.	Yet, for all this, say not that Percy's dead.
	I see a strange confession in thine eye.
	Thou shak'st thy head and hold'st it fear, or sin,
	To speak a truth. If he be slain, say so.
	The tongue offends not that reports his death;
	And he doth sin that doth belie the dead,
	Not he which says the dead is not alive.
	Yet the first bringer of unwelcome news
	Hath but a losing office, and his tongue
	Sounds ever after as a sullen bell,
	Rememb'red tolling a departing friend.
Lord Bardolph.	I cannot think, my lord, your son is dead.
Morton.	I am sorry I should force you to believe
	That which I would to God I had not seen.
	But these mine eyes saw him in bloody state,
	Rend'ring faint quittance, wearied and outbreathed,
	To Harry Monmouth, whose swift wrath beat down
	The never-daunted Percy to the earth,
	From whence with life he never more sprung up.
	In few, his death, whose spirit lent a fire
	Even to the dullest peasant in his camp,
	Being bruited once, took fire and heat away
	From the best-tempered courage in his troops.
	For from his mettle was his party steeled,
	Which once in him abated, all the rest
	Turned on themselves, like dull and heavy lead.
	And as the thing that's heavy in itself,

Upon enforcement flies with greatest speed,
So did our men, heavy in Hotspur's loss,
Lend to this weight such lightness with their fear
That arrows fled not swifter toward their aim
Than did our soldiers, aiming at their safety,
Fly from the field. Then was that noble Worcester
So soon ta'en prisoner. And that furious Scot,
The bloody Douglas, whose well-laboring sword
Had three times slain th' appearance of the King,
'Gan vail his stomach and did grace the shame
Of those that turned their backs, and in his flight,
Stumbling in fear, was took. The sum of all
Is that the King hath won, and hath sent out
A speedy power to encounter you, my lord,
Under the conduct of young Lancaster
And Westmoreland. This is the news at full.

Northumberland. For this I shall have time enough to mourn.
In poison there is physic; and these news,
Having been well, that would have made me sick,
Being sick, have in some measure made me well.
And, as the wretch whose fever-weak'ned joints,
Like strengthless hinges, buckle under life,
Impatient of his fit, breaks like a fire
Out of his keeper's arms, even so my limbs,
Weak'ned with grief, being now enraged with grief,
Are thrice themselves. Hence, therefore, thou nice crutch!
A scaly gauntlet now with joints of steel

Must glove this hand. And hence, thou sickly quoif!
Thou art a guard too wanton for the head
Which princes, fleshed with conquest, aim to hit.
Now bind my brows with iron, and approach
The ragged'st hour that time and spite dare bring
To frown upon th' enraged Northumberland!
Let heaven kiss earth! Now let not Nature's hand
Keep the wild flood confined! Let order die!
And let this world no longer be a stage
To feed contention in a ling'ring act!
But let one spirit of the firstborn Cain
Reign in all bosoms, that, each heart being set
On bloody courses, the rude scene may end,
And darkness be the burier of the dead!

Lord Bardolph. This strained passion doth you wrong, my lord.
Morton. Sweet Earl, divorce not wisdom from your honor.
The lives of all your loving complices
Lean on your health, the which, if you give o'er
To stormy passion, must perforce decay.
You cast th' event of war, my noble lord,
And summed the account of chance, before you said,
"Let us make head." It was your presurmise
That, in the dole of blows, your son might drop.
You knew he walked o'er perils, on an edge,
More likely to fall in than to get o'er.

You were advised his flesh was capable
Of wounds and scars and that his forward spirit
Would lift him where most trade of danger ranged.
Yet did you say, "Go forth." And none of this,
Though strongly apprehended, could restrain
The stiff-borne action. What hath then befall'n,
Or what hath this bold enterprise brought forth,
More than that being which was like to be?

Lord Bardolph. We all that are engaged to this loss
Knew that we ventured on such dangerous seas
That if we wrought out life 'twas ten to one.
And yet we ventured, for the gain proposed
Choked the respect of likely peril feared.
And since we are o'erset, venture again.
Come, we will all put forth, body and goods.

Morton. 'Tis more than time. And, my most noble lord,
I hear for certain, and dare speak the truth:
The gentle Archbishop of York is up
With well-appointed pow'rs. He is a man
Who with a double surety binds his followers.
My lord your son had only but the corpse,
But shadows and the shows of men, to fight.
For that same word "rebellion" did divide
The action of their bodies from their souls,
And they did fight with queasiness, constrained,
As men drink potions, that their weapons only
Seemed on our side. But for their spirits and souls,

This word "rebellion," it had froze them up
As fish are in a pond. But now the Bishop
Turns insurrection to religion.
Supposed sincere and holy in his thoughts,
He's followed both with body and with mind,
And doth enlarge his rising with the blood
Of fair King Richard, scraped from Pomfret stones;
Derives from heaven his quarrel and his cause;
Tells them he doth bestride a bleeding land,
Gasping for life under great Bolingbroke;
And more and less do flock to follow him.

Northumberland. I knew of this before; but, to speak truth,
This present grief had wiped it from my mind.
Go in with me, and counsel every man
The aptest way for safety and revenge.
Get posts and letters, and make friends with speed.
Never so few, and never yet more need.

     [*Exeunt*]

[*Enter Sir John Falstaff and Page*]

Falstaff. Sirrah, you giant, what says the doctor to my water?

Page. He said, sir, the water itself was a good healthy water; but, for the party that owed it, he might have moe diseases than he knew for.

Falstaff. Men of all sorts take a pride to gird at me. The brain of this foolish compounded clay, man is not able to invent anything that intends to laughter more than I invent or is invented on me. I am not only witty in myself, but the cause that wit is in other men. I do here walk before thee like a sow that hath overwhelmed all her litter but one. If the Prince put thee into my service for any other reason than to set me off, why then I have no judgment. Thou whoreson mandrake, thou art fitter to be worn in my cap than to wait at my heels. I was never manned with an agate till now, but I will inset you neither in gold nor silver, but in vile apparel, and send you back again to your master, for a jewel—the juvenal, the Prince your master, whose chin is not yet fledge. I will sooner have a beard grow in the palm of my hand than he shall get one off his cheek, and yet he will not stick to say his face is a face-royal. God may finish it when he will, 'tis not a hair amiss yet. He may keep it still at a face-royal, for a barber shall never earn sixpence out of it; and yet he'll be crowing as if he had writ man ever since his father was a bachelor. He may keep his own grace, but he's almost out of mine, I can assure him. What said Master Dummelton about the satin for my short cloak and my slops?

Page. He said, sir, you should procure him better assurance than Bardolph. He would not take his band and yours; he liked not the security.

Falstaff. Let him be damned, like the glutton! Pray God his tongue be hotter! A whoreson Achitophel! A rascal, yea-forsooth knave! To bear a gentleman in hand, and then stand upon security! The whoreson smooth-pates do now wear nothing but high shoes, and bunches of keys at their girdles; and if a man is through with them in honest taking up, then they must stand upon security. I had as lief they would put ratsbane in my mouth as offer to stop it with "security." I looked 'a should have sent me two-and-twenty yards of satin, as I am a true knight, and he sends me "security." Well, he may sleep in security, for he hath the horn of abundance, and the lightness of his wife shines through it. And yet cannot he see, though he have his own lanthorn to light him. Where's Bardolph?

Page.	He's gone into Smithfield to buy your worship a horse.
Falstaff.	I bought him in Paul's, and he'll buy me a horse in Smithfield. And I could get me but a wife in the stews, I were manned, horsed, and wived.

[*Enter Lord Chief Justice and Servant*]

Page.	Sir, here comes the nobleman that committed the Prince for striking him about Bardolph.
Falstaff.	Wait close — I will not see him.
Chief Justice.	What's he that goes there?
Servant.	Falstaff, and't please your lordship.
Chief Justice.	He that was in question for the robb'ry?
Servant.	He, my lord. But he hath since done good service at Shrewsbury, and, as I hear, is now going with some charge to the Lord John of Lancaster.
Chief Justice.	What, to York? Call him back again.
Servant.	Sir John Falstaff!
Falstaff.	Boy, tell him I am deaf.
Page.	You must speak louder; my master is deaf.
Chief Justice.	I am sure he is — to the hearing of anything good. Go, pluck him by the elbow. I must speak with him.
Servant.	Sir John!

Falstaff.	What! A young knave, and begging! Is there not wars? Is there not employment? Doth not the King lack subjects? Do not the rebels need soldiers? Though it be a shame to be on any side but one, it is worse shame to beg than to be on the worst side, were it worse than the name of rebellion can tell how to make it.
Servant.	You mistake me, sir.
Falstaff.	Why, sir, did I say you were an honest man? Setting my knighthood and my soldiership aside, I had lied in my throat if I had said so.
Servant.	I pray you, sir, then set your knighthood and your soldiership aside and give me leave to tell you you lie in your throat if you say I am any other than an honest man.
Falstaff.	I give thee leave to tell me so! I lay aside that which grows to me! If thou get'st any leave of me, hang me. If thou tak'st leave, thou wert better be hanged. You hunt counter. Hence! Avaunt!
Servant.	Sir, my lord would speak with you.
Chief Justice.	Sir John Falstaff, a word with you.
Falstaff.	My good lord! God give your lordship good time of day. I am glad to see your lordship abroad. I heard say your lordship was sick. I hope your lordship goes abroad by advice. Your lordship, though not clean past your youth, hath yet some smack of an age in you, some relish of the saltness of time in you; and I most humbly beseech your lordship to have a reverent care of your health.
Chief Justice.	Sir John, I sent for you before your expedition to Shrewsbury.
Falstaff.	And't please your lordship, I hear his Majesty is returned with some discomfort from Wales.
Chief Justice.	I talk not of his Majesty. You would not come when I sent for you.
Falstaff.	And I hear, moreover, his Highness is fall'n into this same whoreson apoplexy.
Chief Justice.	Well, God mend him! I pray you, let me speak with you.
Falstaff.	This apoplexy, as I take it, is a kind of lethargy, and't please your lordship, a kind of sleeping in the blood, a whoreson tingling.

Chief Justice.	What, tell you me of it? Be it as it is.
Falstaff.	It hath it original from much grief, from study and perturbation of the brain. I have read the cause of his effects in Galen. It is a kind of deafness.
Chief Justice.	I think you are fall'n into the disease, for you hear not what I say to you.
Falstaff.	Very well, my lord, very well. Rather, and't please you, it is the disease of not listening, the malady of not marking, that I am troubled withal.
Chief Justice.	To punish you by the heels would amend the attention of your ears, and I care not if I do become your physician.
Falstaff.	I am as poor as Job, my lord, but not so patient. Your lordship may minister the potion of imprisonment to me in respect of poverty; but how I should be your patient to follow your prescriptions, the wise may make some dram of a scruple, or indeed a scruple itself.
Chief Justice.	I sent for you, when there were matters against you for your life, to come speak with me.
Falstaff.	As I was then advised by my learned counsel in the laws of this land-service, I did not come.
Chief Justice.	Well, the truth is, Sir John, you live in great infamy.
Falstaff.	He that buckles himself in my belt cannot live in less.
Chief Justice.	Your means are very slender and your waste is great.
Falstaff.	I would it were otherwise. I would my means were greater and my waist slender.
Chief Justice.	You have misled the youthful Prince.
Falstaff.	The young Prince hath misled me. I am the fellow with the great belly, and he my dog.
Chief Justice.	Well, I am loath to gall a new-healed wound. Your day's service at Shrewsbury hath a little gilded over your night's exploit on Gad's Hill. You may thank th' unquiet time for your quiet o'erposting that action.
Falstaff.	My lord?

Chief Justice.	But since all is well, keep it so. Wake not a sleeping wolf.
Falstaff.	To wake a wolf is as bad as smell a fox.
Chief Justice.	What! You are as a candle, the better part burnt out.
Falstaff.	A wassail candle, my lord, all tallow. If I did say of wax, my growth would approve the truth.
Chief Justice.	There is not a white hair in your face but should have his effect of gravity.
Falstaff.	His effect of gravy, gravy, gravy.
Chief Justice.	You follow the young Prince up and down like his ill angel.
Falstaff.	Not so, my lord. Your ill angel is light, but I hope he that looks upon me will take me without weighing. And yet, in some respects, I grant, I cannot go. I cannot tell. Virtue is of so little regard in these costermongers' times that true valor is turned berod. Pregnancy is made a tapster, and hath his quick wit wasted in giving reckonings. All the other gifts appertinent to man, as the malice of this age shapes them, are not worth a gooseberry. You that are old consider not the capacities of us that are young. You do measure the heat of our livers with the bitterness of your galls. And we that are in the vaward of our youth, I must confess, are wags too.
Chief Justice.	Do you set down your name in the scroll of youth, that are written down old with all the characters of age? Have you not a moist eye, a dry hand, a yellow cheek, a white beard, a decreasing leg, an increasing belly? Is not your voice broken, your wind short, your chin double, your wit single, and every part about you blasted with antiquity, and will you yet call yourself young? Fie, fie, fie, Sir John!
Falstaff.	My lord, I was born about three of the clock in the afternoon, with a white head and something a round belly. For my voice, I have lost it with hallowing and singing of anthems. To approve my youth further, I will not. The truth is, I am only old in judgment and understanding; and he that will caper with me for a

thousand marks, let him lend me the money, and have at him! For the box of the ear that the Prince gave you, he gave it like a rude prince, and you took it like a sensible lord, I have checked him for it, and the young lion repents, marry, not in ashes and sackcloth, but in new silk and old sack.

Chief Justice. Well, God send the Prince a better companion!

Falstaff. God send the companion a better prince! I cannot rid my hands of him.

Chief Justice. Well, the King hath severed you and Prince Harry. I hear you are going with Lord John of Lancaster against the Archbishop and the Earl of Northumberland.

Falstaff. Yea, I thank your pretty sweet wit for it. But look you pray, all you that kiss my lady Peace at home, that our armies join not in a hot day, for, by the Lord, I take but two shirts out with me, and I mean not to sweat extraordinarily. If it be a hot day, and I brandish anything but a bottle, I would I might never spit white again. There is not a dangerous action can peep out his head but I am thrust upon it. Well, I cannot last ever. But it was alway yet the trick of our English nation, if they have a good thing, to make it too common. If ye will needs say I am an old man, you should give me rest. I would to God my name were not so terrible to the enemy as it is. I were better to be eaten to death with a rust than to be scoured to nothing with perpetual motion.

Chief Justice. Well, be honest, be honest, and God bless your expedition!

Falstaff. Will your lordship lend me a thousand pound to furnish me forth?

Chief Justice. Not a penny, not a penny. You are too impatient to bear crosses. Fare you well. Commend me to my cousin Westmoreland.

    [*Exeunt Chief Justice and Servant*]

Falstaff. If I do, fillip me with a three-man beetle. A man can no more separate age and covetousness than 'a can part young limbs and lechery. But the gout galls the one and the pox pinches the other, and so both the degrees prevent my curses. Boy!

Page. Sir?

Falstaff.	What money is in my purse?
Page.	Seven groats and twopence.
Falstaff.	I can get no remedy against this consumption of the purse. Borrowing only lingers and lingers it out, but the disease is incurable. Go bear this letter to my Lord of Lancaster, this to the Prince, this to the Earl of Westmoreland, and this to old Mistress Ursula, whom I have weekly sworn to marry since I perceived the first white hair of my chin. About it. You know where to find me. *[Exit Page]* A pox of this gout! Or a gout of this pox! For the one or the other plays the rogue with my great toe. 'Tis no matter if I do halt—I have the wars for my color, and my pension shall seem the more reasonable. A good wit will make use of anything. I will turn diseases to commodity.

       [Exit]

[Enter the Archbishop, Thomas Mowbray,
the Lord Hastings and the Lord Bardolph]

Archbishop. Thus have you heard our cause and known our means;

And, my most noble friends, I pray you all,

Speak plainly your opinions of our hopes.

And first, Lord Marshal, what say you to it?

Mowbray. I well allow the occasion of our arms,

But gladly would be better satisfied

How in our means we should advance ourselves

To look with forehead bold and big enough

Upon the power and puissance of the King.

Hastings. Our present musters grow upon the file

To five-and-twenty thousand men of choice;

And our supplies live largely in the hope

Of great Northumberland, whose bosom burns

With an incensed fire of injuries.

Lord Bardolph. The question then, Lord Hastings, standeth thus:

Whether our present five-and-twenty thousand

May hold up head without Northumberland?

Hastings. With him, we may.

Lord Bardolph.	Yea, marry, there's the point.
	But if without him we be thought too feeble,
	My judgment is, we should not step too far
	Till we had his assistance by the hand.
	For in a theme so bloody-faced as this,
	Conjecture, expectation, and surmise
	Of aids incertain should not be admitted.
Archbishop.	'Tis very true, Lord Bardolph, for indeed
	It was young Hotspur's case at Shrewsbury.
Lord Bardolph.	It was, my lord, who lined himself with hope,
	Eating the air and promise of supply,
	Flatt'ring himself in project of a power
	Much smaller than the smallest of his thoughts,
	And so, with great imagination
	Proper to madmen, led his powers to death
	And, winking, leaped into destruction.
Hastings.	But, by your leave, it never yet did hurt
	To lay down likelihoods and forms of hope.

Lord Bardolph.   Yes, if this present quality of war.
                     Indeed the instant action, a cause on foot,
                     Lives so in hope as in an early spring
                     We see th' appearing buds, which to prove fruit,
                     Hope gives not so much warrant as despair
                     That frosts will bite them. When we mean to build,
                     We first survey the plot, then draw the model.
                     And when we see the figure of the house,
                     Then must we rate the cost of the erection,
                     Which if we find outweighs ability,
                     What do we then but draw anew the model
                     In fewer offices, or at least desist
                     To build at all? Much more, in this great work,
                     Which is almost to pluck a kingdom down.
                     And set another up, should we survey
                     The plot of situation and the model,
                     Consent upon a sure foundation,
                     Question surveyors, know our own estate,
                     How able such a work to undergo,
                     To weigh against his opposite. Or else
                     We fortify in paper and in figures,
                     Using the names of men instead of men,
                     Like one that draws the model of an house
                     Beyond his power to build it, who, half through,
                     Gives o'er and leaves his part-created cost
                     A naked subject to the weeping clouds
                     And waste for churlish winter's tyranny.

Hastings.	Grant that our hopes, yet likely of fair birth,
	Should be stillborn, and that we now possessed
	The utmost man of expectation,
	I think we are so, body strong enough
	Even as we are, to equal with the King.
Lord Bardolph.	What, is the King but five-and-twenty thousand?
Hastings.	To us no more, nay, not so much, Lord Bardolph.
	For his divisions, as the times do brawl,
	Are in three heads: one power against the French,
	And one against Glendower, perforce a third
	Must take up us. So is the unfirm king
	In three divided, and his coffers sound
	With hollow poverty and emptiness.
Archbishop.	That he should draw his several strengths together
	And come against us in full puissance
	Need not to be dreaded.
Hastings.	If he should do so,
	He leaves his back unarmed, the French and Welsh
	Baying him at the heels. Never fear that.
Lord Bardolph.	Who is it like should lead his forces hither?
Hastings.	The Duke of Lancaster and Westmoreland.
	Against the Welsh, himself and Harry Monmouth.
	But who is substituted against the French,
	I have no certain notice.

Archbishop.   Let us on,
               And publish the occasion of our arms.
               The commonwealth is sick of their own choice;
               Their overgreedy love hath surfeited.
               An habitation giddy and unsure
               Hath he that buildeth on the vulgar heart.
               O thou fond many, with what loud applause
               Didst thou beat heaven with blessing Bolingbroke,
               Before he was what thou wouldst have him be!
               And being now trimmed in thine own desires,
               Thou, beastly feeder, art so full of him
               That thou provok'st thyself to cast him up.
               So, so, thou common dog, didst thou disgorge
               Thy glutton bosom of the royal Richard;
               And now thou wouldst eat thy dead vomit up,
               And howl'st to find it. What trust is in these times?
               They that when Richard lived would have him die
               Are now become enamored on his grave.
               Thou that threw'st dust upon his goodly head
               When through proud London he came sighing on
               After th' admired heels of Bolingbroke
               Criest now, "O earth, yield us that king again,
               And take thou this!" O thoughts of men accursed!
               "Past and to come seems best, things present worst."
Mowbray.   Shall we go draw our numbers and set on?
Hastings.   We are time's subjects, and time bids be gone.
                    [Exeunt]

PART II ACT TWO

*[Enter the Hostess of the Tavern and an Officer
or two, Fang and another, followed by Snare]*

Hostess.	Master Fang, have you ent'red the action?
Fang.	It is ent'red.
Hostess.	Where's your yeoman? Is't a lusty yeoman? Will 'a stand to't?
Fang.	Sirrah—where's Snare?
Hostess.	O Lord, ay! Good Master Snare!
Snare.	Here, here.
Fang.	Snare, we must arrest Sir John Falstaff.
Hostess.	Yea, good Master Snare, I have ent'red him and all.
Snare.	It may chance cost some of us our lives, for he will stab.
Hostess.	Alas the day! Take heed of him. He stabbed me in mine own house, and that most beastly. In good faith, 'a cares not what mischief he does, if his weapon be out. He will foin like any devil; he will spare neither man, woman, nor child.
Fang.	If I can close with him, I care not for his thrust.
Hostess.	No, nor I neither. I'll be at your elbow.
Fang.	And I but fist him once, and 'a come but within my vice—
Hostess.	I am undone by his going. I warrant you, he's an infinitive thing upon my score. Good Master Fang, hold him sure. Good Master Snare, let him not 'scape. 'A comes continuantly to Pie Corner—saving your manhoods—to buy a saddle; and he is indited to dinner to the Lubber's Head in Lumbert Street, to Master Smooth's the silkman. I pray you, since my exion is ent'red and my case so openly known to the world, let him be brought in to his answer. A hundred mark is a long one for a poor lone woman to bear, and I have borne, and borne, and borne, and have been fubbed off, and fubbed off, and fubbed off, from this

day to that day, that it is a shame to be thought on. There is no honesty in such dealing, unless a woman should be made an ass and a beast, to bear every knave's wrong. Yonder he comes, and that arrant malmsey-nose knave, Bardolph, with him. Do your offices, do your offices. Master Fang and Master Snare, do me, do me, do me your offices.

[Enter Sir John and Bardolph, and the Boy]

Falstaff. How now! Whose mare's dead? What's the matter?

Fang. Sir John, I arrest you at the suit of Mistress Quickly.

Falstaff. Away, varlets! Draw, Bardolph! Cut me off the villain's head. Throw the quean in the channel.

Hostess. Throw me in the channel! I'll throw thee in the channel. Wilt thou? Wilt thou? Thou bastardly rogue! Murder, murder! Ah, thou honeysuckle villain! Wilt thou kill God's officers and the King's? Ah, thou honeyseed rogue! Thou art a honeyseed, a man-queller, and a woman-queller.

Falstaff. Keep them off, Bardolph.

Fang. A rescue! A rescue!

Hostess. Good people, bring a rescue or two. Thou wo't, wo't thou? Thou wo't, wo't ta? Do, do, thou rogue! Do, thou hempseed!

Page. Away, you scullion! You rampallian! You fustilarian! I'll tickle your catastrophe.

[Enter Lord Chief Justice and his Men]

Chief Justice. What is the matter? Keep the peace here, ho!

Hostess. Good my lord, be good to me. I beseech you, stand to me.

Chief Justice. How now, Sir John! What are you brawling here? Doth this become your place, your time and business? You should have been well on your way to York. Stand from him, fellow. Wherefore hang'st thou upon him?

Hostess. O my most worshipful lord, and't please your Grace, I am a poor widow of Eastcheap, and he is arrested at my suit.

Chief Justice.	For what sum?
Hostess.	It is more than for some, my lord, it is for all I have. He hath eaten me out of house and home; he hath put all my substance into that fat belly of his. But I will have some of it out again, or I will ride thee o' nights like the mare.
Falstaff.	I think I am as like to ride the mare, if I have any vantage of ground to get up.
Chief Justice.	How comes this, Sir John? What man of good temper would endure this tempest of exclamation? Are you not ashamed to enforce a poor widow to so rough a course to come by her own?
Falstaff.	What is the gross sum that I owe thee?
Hostess.	Marry, if thou wert an honest man, thyself and the money too. Thou didst swear to me upon a parcel-gilt goblet, sitting in my Dolphin chamber, at the round table, by a sea-coal fire, upon Wednesday in Wheeson week, when the Prince broke thy head for liking his father to a singing-man of Windsor, thou didst swear to me then, as I was washing thy wound, to marry me and make me my lady thy wife. Canst thou deny it? Did not goodwife Keech, the butcher's wife, come in then and call me gossip Quickly? Coming in to borrow a mess of vinegar, telling us she had a good dish of prawns, whereby thou didst desire to eat some, whereby I told thee they were ill for a green wound? And didst thou not, when she was gone downstairs, desire me to be no more so familiarity with such poor people, saying that ere long they should call me "Madam"? And didst thou not kiss me and bid me fetch thee thirty shillings? I put thee now to thy book-oath. Deny it, if thou canst.
Falstaff.	My lord, this is a poor mad soul, and she says up and down the town that her eldest son is like you. She hath been in good case, and the truth is, poverty hath distracted her. But for these foolish officers, I beseech you I may have redress against them.
Chief Justice.	Sir John, Sir John, I am well acquainted with your manner of wrenching the true cause the false way. It is not a confident brow, nor the throng of words that come

with such more than impudent sauciness from you, can thrust me from a level consideration. You have, as it appears to me, practiced upon the easy-yielding spirit of this woman, and made her serve your uses both in purse and in person.

Hostess. Yea, in truth, my lord.

Chief Justice. Pray thee, peace. Pay her the debt you owe her and unpay the villainy you have done with her. The one you may do with sterling money, and the other with current repentance.

Falstaff. My lord, I will not undergo this sneap without reply. You call honorable boldness impudent sauciness. If a man will make curtsy and say nothing, he is virtuous. No, my lord, my humble duty rememb'red, I will not be your suitor. I say to you, I do desire deliverance from these officers, being upon hasty employment in the King's affairs.

Chief Justice. You speak as having power to do wrong. But answer in th' effect of your reputation, and satisfy the poor woman.

Falstaff. Come hither, hostess.

[*Enter a Messenger, Gower*]

Chief Justice. Now, Master Gower, what news?

Gower. The King, my lord, and Harry Prince of Wales
Are near at hand. The rest the paper tells.

[*They draw aside*]

Falstaff. [*To Hostess*] As I am a gentleman!

Hostess. Faith, you said so before.

Falstaff. As I am a gentleman, come, no more words of it.

Hostess. By this heavenly ground I tread on, I must be fain to pawn both my plate and the tapestry of my dining chambers.

Falstaff. Glasses, glasses, is the only drinking. And for thy walls, a pretty slight drollery, or the story of the Prodigal, or the German hunting in waterwork, is worth a thousand of these bed-hangers and these fly-bitten tapestries. Let it be ten pound, if thou canst. Come, and 'twere not for thy humors, there's not a better wench in England. Go, wash thy face, and draw the action. Come, thou must not be in this humor with me. Dost not know me? Come, come, I know thou wast set on to this.

Hostess. Pray thee, Sir John, let it be but twenty nobles. I' faith, I am loath to pawn my plate, so God save me, la!

Falstaff. Let it alone; I'll make other shift. You'll be a fool still.

Hostess. Well, you shall have it, though I pawn my gown. I hope you'll come to supper. You'll pay me all together?

Falstaff. Will I live? [*To Bardolph*] Go, with her, with her. Hook on, hook on!

Hostess. Will you have Doll Tearsheet meet you at supper?

Falstaff. No more words. Let's have her.

     [*Exit Hostess and Sergeant*
      Fang, Bardolph and others]

Chief Justice. [*To Gower*] I have heard better news.

Falstaff. What's the news, my lord?

Chief Justice. [*Ignoring Falstaff*] Where lay the King tonight?

Gower. At Basingstoke, my lord.

Falstaff. I hope, my lord, all's well. What is the news, my lord?

Chief Justice. Come all his forces back?

Gower.   No. Fifteen hundred foot, five hundred horse,
     Are marched up to my Lord of Lancaster,
     Against Northumberland and the Archbishop.

Falstaff.   Comes the King back from Wales, my noble lord?

Chief Justice.   [*To his men*] You shall have letters of me presently.
     Come, go along with me, good Master Gower.

Falstaff.	My lord!
Chief Justice.	What's the matter?
Falstaff.	Master Gower, shall I entreat you with me to dinner?
Gower.	I must wait upon my good lord here, I thank you, good Sir John.
Chief Justice.	Sir John, you loiter here too long, being you are to take soldiers up in counties as you go.
Falstaff.	Will you sup with me, Master Gower?
Chief Justice.	What foolish master taught you these manners, Sir John?
Falstaff.	Master Gower, if they become me not, he was a fool that taught them me. This is the right fencing grace, my lord—tap for tap, and so part fair.
Chief Justice.	Now the Lord lighten thee! Thou art a great fool.

[*Exeunt*]

[Enter Prince Henry, Poins, with others]

Prince. Trust me, I am exceeding weary.

Poins. Is't come to that? I had thought weariness durst not have attached one of so high blood.

Prince. Faith, it does me, though it discolors the complexion of my greatness to acknowledge it. Doth it not show vilely in me to desire small beer?

Poins. Why, a prince should not be so loosely studied as to remember so weak a composition.

Prince. Belike, then, my appetite was not princely got, for, by my troth, I do now remember the poor creature, small beer. But indeed these humble considerations make me out of love with my greatness. What a disgrace is it to me to remember thy name! Or to know thy face tomorrow! Or to take note how many pair of silk stockings thou hast, viz. these, and those that were thy peach-colored ones! Or to bear the inventory of thy shirts, as: one for superfluity and another for use! But that the tenniscourt-keeper knows better than I; for it is a low ebb of linen with thee when thou keepest not racket there, as thou hast not done a great while, because the rest of thy low countries have made a shift to eat up thy holland. And God knows whether those that bawl out the ruins of thy linen shall inherit His kingdom. But the midwives say the children are not in the fault, whereupon the world increases, and kindreds are mightily strengthened.

Poins. How ill it follows, after you have labored so hard, you should talk so idly! Tell me, how many good young princes would do so, their fathers being so sick as yours at this time is?

Prince. Shall I tell thee one thing, Poins?

Poins. Yes, faith, and let it be an excellent good thing.

Prince.	It shall serve among wits of no higher breeding than thine.
Poins.	Go to. I stand the push of your one thing that you will tell.
Prince.	Marry, I tell thee, it is not meet that I should be sad, now my father is sick. Albeit I could tell to thee, as to one it pleases me, for fault of a better, to call my friend, I could be sad, and sad indeed, too.
Poins.	Very hardly upon such a subject.
Prince.	By this hand, thou thinkest me as far in the devil's book as thou and Falstaff for obduracy and persistency. Let the end try the man. But I tell thee, my heart bleeds inwardly that my father is so sick. And keeping such vile company as thou art hath in reason taken from me all ostentation of sorrow.
Poins.	The reason?
Prince.	What wouldst thou think of me if I should weep?
Poins.	I would think thee a most princely hypocrite.
Prince.	It would be every man's thought, and thou art a blessed fellow to think as every man thinks. Never a man's thought in the world keeps the roadway better than thine. Every man would think me an hypocrite indeed. And what accites your most worshipful thought to think so?
Poins.	Why, because you have been so lewd and so much engraffed to Falstaff.
Prince.	And to thee.
Poins.	By this light, I am well spoke on; I can hear it with mine own ears. The worst that they can say of me is that I am a second brother and that I am a proper fellow of my hands, and those two things I confess I cannot help. By the mass, here comes Bardolph.

[Enter Bardolph and Boy Page]

Prince.	And the boy that I gave Falstaff. 'A had him from me Christian, and look if the fat villain have not transformed him ape.
Bardolph.	God save your Grace.

Prince.	And yours, most noble Bardolph.
Poins.	Come, you virtuous ass, you bashful fool, must you be blushing? Wherefore blush you now? What a maidenly man-at-arms are you become! Is't such a matter to get a pottle-pot's maidenhead?
Page.	'A calls me e'en now, my lord, through a red lattice, and I could discern no part of his face from the window. At last I spied his eyes, and methought he had made two holes in the ale-wife's petticoat and so peeped through.
Prince.	Has not the boy profited?
Bardolph.	Away, you whoreson upright rabbit, away!
Page.	Away, you rascally Althaea's dream, away!
Prince.	Instruct us, boy. What dream, boy?
Page.	Marry, my lord, Althaea dreamed she was delivered of a firebrand, and therefore I call him her dream.
Prince.	A crown's worth of good interpretation. There 'tis, boy. [*Tips him*]
Poins.	O, that this blossom could be kept from cankers! Well, there is sixpence to preserve thee.
Bardolph.	And you do not make him hanged among you, the gallows shall have wrong.
Prince.	And how doth thy master, Bardolph?
Bardolph.	Well, my lord. He heard of your Grace's coming to town. There's a letter for you.
Poins.	Delivered with good respect. And how doth the martlemas, your master?
Bardolph.	In bodily health, sir.
Poins.	Marry, the immortal part needs a physician, but that moves not him. Though that be sick, it dies not.
Prince.	I do allow this wen to be as familiar with me as my dog, and he holds his place, for look you how he writes.
Poins.	[*Reads*] "John Falstaff, knight"—every man must know that, as oft as he has occasion to name himself. Even like those that are kin to the King, for they never

prick their finger but they say, "There's some of the King's blood spilt." "How comes that?" says he that takes upon him not to conceive. The answer is as ready as a borrowed cap, "I am the King's poor cousin, sir."

Prince. Nay, they will be kin to us, or they will fetch it from Japhet. But the letter.
[Reads] "Sir John Falstaff, knight, to the son of the King nearest his father, Harry Prince of Wales, greeting."

Poins. Why, this is a certificate.

Prince. Peace! [Reads] "I will imitate the honorable Romans in brevity."

Poins. He sure means brevity in breath, short-winded.

Prince. [Reads] "I commend me to thee, I commend thee, and I leave thee. Be not too familiar with Poins, for he misuses thy favors so much that he swears thou art to marry his sister Nell. Repent at idle times as thou mayst, and so farewell.
"Thine, by yea and no, which is as much as to say, as thou usest him, JACK FALSTAFF with my familiars, JOHN with my brothers and sisters, and SIR JOHN with all Europe."

Poins. My lord, I'll steep this letter in sack and make him eat it.

Prince. That's to make him eat twenty of his words. But do you use me thus, Ned? Must I marry your sister?

Poins. God send the wench no worse fortune! But I never said so.

Prince. Well, thus we play the fools with the time, and the spirits of the wise sit in the clouds and mock us. Is your master here in London?

Bardolph. Yea, my lord.

Prince. Where sups he? Doth the old boar feed in the old frank?

Bardolph. At the old place, my lord, in Eastcheap.

Prince. What company?

Page. Ephesians, my lord, of the old church.

Prince. Sup any women with him?

Page.	None, my lord, but old Mistress Quickly and Mistress Doll Tearsheet.
Prince.	What pagan may that be?
Page.	A proper gentlewoman, sir, and a kinswoman of my master's.
Prince.	Even such kin as the parish heifers are to the town bull. Shall we steal upon them, Ned, at supper?
Poins.	I am your shadow, my lord; I'll follow you.
Prince.	Sirrah, you boy, and Bardolph, no word to your master that I am yet come to town. There's for your silence. [*Tips them*]
Bardolph.	I have no tongue, sir.
Page.	And for mine, sir, I will govern it.
Prince.	Fare you well; go.
	[*Exeunt Bardolph and Page*]
	This Doll Tearsheet should be some road.
Poins.	I warrant you, as common as the way between Saint Alban's and London.
Prince.	How might we see Falstaff bestow himself tonight in his true colors, and not ourselves be seen?
Poins.	Put on two leathern jerkins and aprons, and wait upon him at his table as drawers.
Prince.	From a God to a bull? A heavy descension! It was Jove's case. From a prince to a prentice? A low transformation! That shall be mine, for in everything the purpose must weigh with the folly. Follow me, Ned.
	[*Exeunt*]

[Enter Northumberland, his wife, Lady Northum-
berland, and the wife to Harry Percy, Lady Percy]

Northumberland. I pray thee, loving wife, and gentle daughter,
Give even way unto my rough affairs.
Put not you on the visage of the times
And be like them to Percy troublesome.

Lady Northumberland. I have given over; I will speak no more.
Do what you will, your wisdom be your guide.

Northumberland. Alas, sweet wife, my honor is at pawn,
And, but my going, nothing can redeem it.

Lady Percy. O yet, for God's sake, go not to these wars!
The time was, father, that you broke your word,
When you were more endeared to it than now,
When your own Percy, when my heart's dear Harry,
Threw many a northward look to see his father
Bring up his powers, but he did long in vain.
Who then persuaded you to stay at home?
There were two honors lost, yours and your son's.
For yours, the God of heaven brighten it!
For his, it stuck upon him as the sun
In the gray vault of heaven, and by his light
Did all the chivalry of England move
To do brave acts. He was indeed the glass
Wherein the noble youth did dress themselves.
He had no legs that practiced not his gait;

And speaking thick, which nature made his blemish,
Became the accents of the valiant,
For those that could speak low and tardily
Would turn their own perfection to abuse,
To seem like him. So that in speech, in gait,
In diet, in affections of delight,
In military rules, humors of blood,
He was the mark and glass, copy and book,
That fashioned others. And him! O wondrous! Him!
O miracle of men! Him did you leave,
Second to none, unseconded by you,
To look upon the hideous god of war
In disadvantage, to abide a field
Where nothing but the sound of Hotspur's name
Did seem defensible. So you left him.
Never, O never, do his ghost the wrong
To hold your honor more precise and nice
With others than with him! Let them alone.
The Marshal and the Archbishop are strong.
Had my sweet Harry had but half their numbers,
Today might I, hanging on Hotspur's neck,
Have talked of Monmouth's grave.

Northumberland.	Beshrew your heart,
	Fair daughter, you do draw my spirits from me
	With new lamenting ancient oversights.
	But I must go and meet with danger there,
	Or it will seek me in another place
	And find me worse provided.
Lady Northumberland.	O, fly to Scotland,
	Till that the nobles and the armed commons
	Have of their puissance made a little taste.
Lady Percy.	If they get ground and vantage of the King,
	Then join you with them, like a rib of steel,
	To make strength stronger. But, for all our loves,
	First let them try themselves. So did your son;
	He was so suff'red. So came I a widow,
	And never shall have length of life enough
	To rain upon remembrance with mine eyes,
	That it may grow and sprout as high as heaven,
	For recordation to my noble husband.
Northumberland.	Come, come, go in with me. 'Tis with my mind
	As with the tide swelled up unto his height,
	That makes a still-stand, running neither way.
	Fain would I go to meet the Archbishop,
	But many thousand reasons hold me back.
	I will resolve for Scotland. There am I,
	Till time and vantage crave my company.

        [Exeunt]

SCENE IV

MISTRESS QUICKLY'S TAVERN

[Enter a Drawer or two, Francis and another]

Francis. What the devil hast thou brought there? Apple-johns? Thou knowest Sir John cannot endure an apple-john.

Drawer. Mass, thou say'st true. The Prince once set a dish of apple-johns before him, and told him there were five more Sir Johns, and, putting off his hat, said, "I will now take my leave of these six dry, round, old, withered knights." It ang'red him to the heart. But he hath forgot that.

Francis. Why, then, cover, and set them down. And see if thou canst find out Sneak's noise. Mistress Tearsheet would fain hear some music.

[Enter Will, a third Drawer]

Will. Dispatch! The room where they supped is too hot. They'll come in straight.

Francis. Sirrah, here will be the Prince and Master Poins anon, and they will put on two of our jerkins and aprons, and Sir John must not know of it. Bardolph hath brought word.

Drawer. By the mass, here will be old Utis. It will be an excellent stratagem.

Francis. I'll see if I can find out Sneak. *[Exit]*

[Enter Mistress Quickly, the Hostess, and Doll Tearsheet]

Hostess. I' faith, sweetheart, methinks now you are in an excellent good temperality. Your pulsidge beats as extraordinarily as heart would desire, and your color, I warrant you, is as red as any rose, in good truth, la! But, i' faith, you have drunk too much canaries, and that's a marvelous searching wine, and it perfumes the blood ere one can say, "What's this?" How do you now?

Doll. Better than I was. Hem!

Hostess. Why, that's well said. A good heart's worth gold. Lo, here comes Sir John.

[Enter Sir John Falstaff]

Falstaff. *[Sings]* "When Arthur first in court"—Empty the jordan!—"And was a worthy king."—How now, Mistress Doll!

Hostess. Sick of a calm, yea, good faith.

Falstaff. So is all her sect. And they be once in a calm, they are sick.

Doll. A pox damn you, you muddy rascal, is that all the comfort you give me?

Falstaff. You make fat rascals, Mistress Doll.

Doll. I make them? Gluttony and diseases make, I make them not.

Falstaff. If the cook help to make the gluttony, you help to make the diseases, Doll. We catch of you, Doll, we catch of you. Grant that, my poor virtue, grant that.

Doll. Yea, joy, our chains and our jewels.

Falstaff. "Your brooches, pearls, and ouches." For to serve bravely is to come halting off, you know. To come off the breach with his pike bent bravely, and to surgery bravely; to venture upon the charged chambers bravely—

Doll. Hang yourself, you muddy conger, hang yourself!

Hostess. By my troth, this is the old fashion. You two never meet but you fall to some discord. You are both, i' good truth, as rheumatic as two dry toasts. You cannot one bear with another's confirmities. What the goodyear! One must bear, and that must be you. *[To Doll]* You are the weaker vessel, as they say, the emptier vessel.

Doll. Can a weak empty vessel bear such a huge full hogshead? There's a whole merchant's venture of Bordeaux stuff in him. You have not seen a hulk better stuffed in the hold. Come, I'll be friends with thee, Jack. Thou art going to the wars, and whether I shall ever see thee again or no, there is nobody cares.

[Enter Drawer]

Drawer. Sir, Ancient Pistol's below and would speak with you.

Doll. Hang him, swaggering rascal! Let him not come hither. It is the foul-mouthed'st rogue in England.

Hostess.	If he swagger, let him not come here. No, by my faith. I must live among my neighbors. I'll no swaggerers. I am in good name and fame with the very best. Shut the door, there comes no swaggerers here. I have not lived all this while to have swaggering now. Shut the door, I pray you.
Falstaff.	Dost thou hear, hostess?
Hostess.	Pray ye, pacify yourself, Sir John. There comes no swaggerers here.
Falstaff.	Dost thou hear? It is mine Ancient.
Hostess.	Tilly-fally, Sir John, ne'er tell me. And your ancient swagg'rer comes not in my doors. I was before Master Tisick, the debuty, t' other day, and, as he said to me, 'twas no longer ago than Wednesday last, "I' good faith, neighbor Quickly," says he—Master Dumbe, our minister, was by then—"neighbor Quickly," says he, "receive those that are civil, for," said he, "you are in an ill name." Now 'a said so, I can tell whereupon. "For," says he, "you are an honest woman, and well thought on; therefore take heed what guests you receive. Receive," says he, "no swaggering companions." There comes none here. You would bless you to hear what he said. No, I'll no swagg'rers.
Falstaff.	He's no swagg'rer, hostess, a tame cheater, i' faith. You may stroke him as gently as a puppy greyhound. He'll not swagger with a Barbary hen, if her feathers turn back in any show of resistance. Call him up, drawer. [*Exit Drawer*]
Hostess.	Cheater, call you him? I will bar no honest man my house, nor no cheater. But I do not love swaggering, by my troth. I am the worse when one says "swagger." Feel, masters, how I shake, look you, I warrant you.
Doll.	So you do, hostess.
Hostess.	Do I? Yea, in very truth, do I, and 'twere an aspen leaf. I cannot abide swagg'rers.
	[*Enter Ancient Pistol, Bardolph, and his Page*]
Pistol.	God save you, Sir John!

Falstaff.	Welcome, Ancient Pistol. Here, Pistol, I charge you with a cup of sack. Do you discharge upon mine hostess.
Pistol.	I will discharge upon her, Sir John, with two bullets.
Falstaff.	She is pistol-proof, sir; you shall not hardily offend her.
Hostess.	Come, I'll drink no proofs nor no bullets. I'll drink no more than will do me good, for no man's pleasure, I.
Pistol.	Then to you, Mistress Dorothy; I will charge you.
Doll.	Charge me! I scorn you, scurvy companion. What! You poor, base, rascally, cheating, lack-linen mate. Away, you moldy rogue, away! I am meat for your master.
Pistol.	I know you, Mistress Dorothy.
Doll.	Away, you cut-purse rascal! You filthy bung, away! By this wine, I'll thrust my knife in your moldy chaps, and you play the saucy cuttle with me. Away, you bottle-ale rascal! You basket-hilt stale juggler, you! Since when, I pray you, sir? God's light, with two points on your shoulder? Much!
Pistol.	God let me not live but I will murder your ruff for this.
Falstaff.	No more, Pistol; I would not have you go off here. Discharge yourself of our company, Pistol.
Hostess.	No, good Captain Pistol, not here, sweet Captain.
Doll.	Captain! Thou abominable damned cheater, art thou not ashamed to be called Captain? And captains were of my mind, they would truncheon you out for taking their names upon you before you have earned them. You a captain! You slave, for what? For tearing a poor whore's ruff in a bawdy house? He a captain! Hang him, rogue! He lives upon moldy stewed prunes and dried cakes. A captain! God's light, these villains will make the word as odious as the word "occupy," which was an excellent good word before it was ill sorted. Therefore captains had need look to't.
Bardolph.	Pray thee, go down, good Ancient.

Falstaff.	Hark thee hither, Mistress Doll.
Pistol.	Not I! I tell thee what, Corporal Bardolph, I could tear her! I'll be revenged of her!
Page.	Pray thee, go down.
Pistol.	I'll see her damned first, to Pluto's damned lake, by this hand, to th' infernal deep, with Erebus and tortures vile also. Hold hook and line, say I. Down, down, dogs! Down, faitors! Have we not Hiren here?
Hostess.	Good Captain Pizzle, be quiet. 'Tis very late, i' faith. I beseek you now, aggravate your choler.

Pistol.   These be good humors, indeed! Shall packhorses
And hollow pampered jades of Asia,
Which cannot go but thirty mile a day,
Compare with Caesars, and with Cannibals,
And Trojan Greeks? Nay, rather damn them with
King Cerberus, and let the welkin roar.
Shall we fall foul for toys?

Hostess.	By my troth, Captain, these are very bitter words.
Bardolph.	Be gone, good Ancient. This will grow to a brawl anon.
Pistol.	Die men like dogs! Give crowns like pins! Have we not Hiren here?
Hostess.	O' my word, Captain, there's none such here. What the goodyear! Do you think I would deny her? For God's sake, be quiet.

Pistol.   Then feed, and be fat, my fair Calipolis.
Come, give's some sack.
"*Si fortune me tormente, sperato me contento.*"
Fear we broadsides? No, let the fiend give fire.
Give me some sack. And, sweetheart, lie thou there.
[Lays down his sword]
Come we to full points here, and are etceteras no things?

Falstaff.	Pistol, I would be quiet.
Pistol.	Sweet knight, I kiss thy neaf. What! We have seen the seven stars.
Doll.	For God's sake, thrust him downstairs. I cannot endure such a fustian rascal.
Pistol.	Thrust him downstairs! Know we not Galloway nags?
Falstaff.	Quoit him down, Bardolph, like a shove-groat shilling. Nay, and 'a do nothing but speak nothing, 'a shall be nothing here.
Bardolph.	Come, get you downstairs.
Pistol.	What! Shall we have incision? Shall we imbrue?

[Snatches up his sword]

Then death rock me asleep, abridge my doleful days!
Why, then, let grievous, ghastly, gaping wounds
Untwined the Sisters Three! Come, Atropos, I say!

Hostess.	Here's goodly stuff toward!
Falstaff.	Give me my rapier, boy.
Doll.	I pray thee, Jack, I pray thee, do not draw.
Falstaff.	Get you downstairs!

[Draws, and threatens Pistol]

Hostess.	Here's a goodly tumult! I'll forswear keeping house afore I'll be in these tirrits and frights. So, murder, I warrant now. Alas, alas! Put up your naked weapons, put up your naked weapons.

[Falstaff drives Pistol out, Bardolph following]

Doll.	I pray thee, Jack, be quiet. The rascal's gone. Ah, you whoreson little valiant villain, you!
Hostess.	Are you not hurt i' th' groin? Methought 'a made a shrewd thrust at your belly.

[Enter Bardolph]

Falstaff.	Have you turned him out o' doors?
Bardolph.	Yea, sir. The rascal's drunk. You have hurt him, sir, i' th' shoulder.

Falstaff.	A rascal! To brave me!
Doll.	Ah, you sweet little rogue, you! Alas, poor ape, how thou sweat'st! Come, let me wipe thy face. Come on, you whoreson chops. Ah, rogue! I' faith, I love thee. Thou art as valorous as Hector of Troy, worth five of Agamemnon, and ten times better than the Nine Worthies. Ah, villain!
Falstaff.	A rascally slave! I will toss the rogue in a blanket.
Doll.	Do, and thou dar'st for thy heart. And thou dost, I'll canvas thee between a pair of sheets.

      [Enter Musicians]

Page.	The music is come, sir.
Falstaff.	Let them play. Play, sirs. Sit on my knee, Doll. A rascal bragging slave! The rogue fled from me like quicksilver.
Doll.	I' faith *[aside]* and thou followedst him like a church. Thou whoreson little tidy Bartholomew boar-pig, when wilt thou leave fighting o' days and foining o' nights, and begin to patch up thine old body for heaven?

      [Enter Prince and Poins disguised]

Falstaff.	Peace, good Doll! Do not speak like a death's-head. Do not bid me remember mine end.
Doll.	Sirrah, what humor's the Prince of?
Falstaff.	A good shallow young fellow. 'A would have made a good pantler, 'a would ha' chipped bread well.
Doll.	They say Poins has a good wit.
Falstaff.	He a good wit? Hang him, baboon! His wit's as thick as Tewksbury mustard. There's no more conceit in him than is in a mallet.
Doll.	Why does the Prince love him so, then?
Falstaff.	Because their legs are both of a bigness, and 'a plays at quoits well, and eats conger and fennel, and drinks off candles' ends for flap-dragons, and rides the

wild-mare with the boys, and jumps upon joined-stools, and swears with a good grace, and wears his boots very smooth, like unto the Sign of the Leg, and breeds no bate with telling of discreet stories; and such other gambol faculties 'a has, that show a weak mind and an able body, for the which the Prince admits him. For the Prince himself is such another; the weight of a hair will turn scales between their avoirdupois.

Prince. Would not this nave of a wheel have his ears cut off?

Poins. Let's beat him before his whore.

Prince. Look, whe'r the withered elder hath not his poll clawed like a parrot.

Poins. Is it not strange that desire should so many years outlive performance?

Falstaff. Kiss me, Doll.

Prince. Saturn and Venus this year in conjunction! What says th' almanac to that?

Poins. And look whether the fiery Trigon, his man, be not lisping to his master's old tables, his notebook, his counsel-keeper.

Falstaff. Thou dost give me flattering busses.

Doll. By my troth, I kiss thee with a most constant heart.

Falstaff. I am old, I am old.

Doll. I love thee better than I love e'er a scurvy young boy of them all.

Falstaff. What stuff wilt have a kirtle of? I shall receive money o' Thursday. Shalt have a cap tomorrow. A merry song, come. 'A grows late; we'll to bed. Thou'lt forget me when I am gone.

Doll. By my troth, thou'lt set me a-weeping, and thou say'st so. Prove that ever I dress myself handsome till thy return. Well, hearken o' th' end.

Falstaff. Some sack, Francis.

Prince. Poins. Anon, anon, sir.

[Coming forward]

Falstaff. Ha! A bastard son of the King's? And art not thou Poins his brother?

Prince.	Why, thou globe of sinful continents, what a life dost thou lead!
Falstaff.	A better than thou. I am a gentleman, thou art a drawer.
Prince.	Very true, sir, and I come to draw you out by the ears.
Hostess.	O, the Lord preserve thy Grace! By my troth, welcome to London. Now, the Lord bless that sweet face of thine! O Jesu, are you come from Wales?
Falstaff.	Thou whoreson mad compound of majesty, by this light flesh and corrupt blood, thou art welcome.
Doll.	How, you fat fool! I scorn you.
Poins.	My lord, he will drive you out of your revenge and turn all to a merriment, if you take not the heat.
Prince.	You whoreson candle-mine you, how vilely did you speak of me now before this honest, virtuous, civil gentlewoman!
Hostess.	God's blessing of your good heart! And so she is, by my troth.
Falstaff.	Didst thou hear me?
Prince.	Yea, and you knew me, as you did when you ran away by Gad's Hill. You knew I was at your back, and spoke it on purpose to try my patience.
Falstaff.	No, no, no, not so. I did not think thou wast within hearing.
Prince.	I shall drive you then to confess the willful abuse, and then I know how to handle you.
Falstaff.	No abuse, Hal, o' mine honor, no abuse.
Prince.	Not to dispraise me and call me pantler and bread-chipper and I know not what?
Falstaff.	No abuse, Hal.
Poins.	No abuse?
Falstaff.	No abuse, Ned, i' th' world. Honest Ned, none. I dispraised him before the wicked, that the wicked might not fall in love with thee. In which doing, I have done the part of a careful friend and a true subject, and thy father is to give me thanks for it. No abuse, Hal. None, Ned, none. No, faith, boys, none.

Prince.	See now, whether pure fear and entire cowardice doth not make thee wrong this virtuous gentlewoman to close with us. Is she of the wicked? Is thine hostess here of the wicked? Or is thy boy of the wicked? Or honest Bardolph, whose zeal burns in his nose, of the wicked?
Poins.	Answer, thou dead elm, answer.
Falstaff.	The fiend hath pricked down Bardolph irrecoverable, and his face is Lucifer's privy-kitchen, where he doth nothing but roast malt-worms. For the boy, there is a good angel about him, but the devil blinds him too.
Prince.	For the women?
Falstaff.	For one of them, she's in hell already, and burns poor souls. For th' other, I owe her money, and whether she be damned for that, I know not.
Hostess.	No, I warrant you.
Falstaff.	No, I think thou art not. I think thou art quit for that. Marry, there is another indictment upon thee, for suffering flesh to be eaten in thy house, contrary to the law, for the which I think thou wilt howl.
Hostess.	All victuallers do so. What's a joint of mutton or two in a whole Lent?
Prince.	You, gentlewoman—
Doll.	What says your Grace?
Falstaff.	His Grace says that which his flesh rebels against. [*Peto knocks at door*]
Hostess.	Who knocks so loud at door? Look to th' door there, Francis. [*Enter Peto*]
Prince.	Peto, how now! What news?
Peto.	The King your father is at Westminster, And there are twenty weak and wearied posts Come from the north. And as I came along I met and overtook a dozen captains, Bareheaded, sweating, knocking at the taverns, And asking everyone for Sir John Falstaff.

Prince.	By heaven, Poins, I feel me much to blame,
	So idly to profane the precious time,
	When tempest of commotion, like the south
	Borne with black vapor, doth begin to melt
	And drop upon our bare unarmed heads.
	Give me my sword and cloak. Falstaff, good night.

[*Exeunt Prince and Poins, Peto, and Bardolph*]

Falstaff. Now comes in the sweetest morsel of the night, and we must hence and leave it unpicked. [*Sound of knocking*] More knocking at the door?

[*Enter Bardolph*]

How now! What's the matter?

Bardolph. You must away to court, sir, presently. A dozen captains stay at door for you.

Falstaff. [*To the Page*] Pay the musicians, sirrah. Farewell, hostess. Farewell, Doll. You see, my good wenches, how men of merit are sought after. The undeserver may sleep when the man of action is called on. Farewell, good wenches. If I be not sent away post, I will see you again ere I go.

Doll. I cannot speak. If my heart be not ready to burst—well, sweet Jack, have a care of thyself.

Falstaff. Farewell, farewell.

[*Exit with Bardolph*]

Hostess. Well, fare thee well. I have known thee these twenty-nine years, come peascod-time, but an honester and truer-hearted man—well, fare thee well.

Bardolph. [*Within*] Mistress Tearsheet!

Hostess. What's the matter?

Bardolph. [*Within*] Bid Mistress Tearsheet come to my master.

Hostess. O, run, Doll, run, run, good Doll. Come. [*To Bardolph within*] She comes blubbered. Yea, will you come, Doll? [*Exeunt*]

PART II ACT THREE

[*Enter the King in his nightgown, alone*]

King. [*To a Page, within*] Go, call the Earls of Surrey and of Warwick.
But, ere they come, bid them o'erread these letters
And well consider of them. Make good speed!
How many thousand of my poorest subjects
Are at this hour asleep! O sleep, O gentle sleep,
Nature's soft nurse, how have I frighted thee,
That thou no more wilt weigh my eyelids down
And steep my senses in forgetfulness?
Why rather, sleep, liest thou in smoky cribs,
Upon uneasy pallets stretching thee
And hushed with buzzing night-flies to thy slumber,
Than in the perfumed chambers of the great,
Under the canopies of costly state,
And lulled with sound of sweetest melody?
O thou dull god, why li'st thou with the vile
In loathsome beds, and leavest the kingly couch
A watchcase or a common 'larum-bell?
Wilt thou upon the high and giddy mast
Seal up the ship-boy's eyes, and rock his brains
In cradle of the rude imperious surge
And in the visitation of the winds,
Who take the ruffian billows by the top,
Curling their monstrous heads and hanging them
With deafing clamor in the slippery clouds,

That, with the hurly, death itself awakes?
Canst thou, O partial sleep, give thy repose
To the wet sea-son in an hour so rude,
And in the calmest and most stillest night,
With all appliances and means to boot,
Deny it to a king? Then happy low, lie down!
Uneasy lies the head that wears a crown.

[Enter Warwick, Surrey, and Sir John Blunt]

Warwick. Many good morrows to your Majesty!

King. Is it good morrow, lords?

Warwick. 'Tis one o'clock, and past.

King. Why, then, good morrow to you all, my lords.
Have you read o'er the letter that I sent you?

Warwick. We have, my liege.

King. Then you perceive the body of our kingdom
How foul it is, what rank diseases grow,
And with what danger, near the heart of it.

Warwick. It is but as a body yet distempered,
Which to his former strength may be restored
With good advice and little medicine.
My Lord Northumberland will soon be cooled.

King. O God, that one might read the book of fate,
And see the revolution of the times
Make mountains level, and the continent,
Weary of solid firmness, melt itself
Into the sea! And other times to see
The beachy girdle of the ocean
Too wide for Neptune's hips. How chances, mocks,
And changes fill the cup of alteration
With divers liquors! O, if this were seen,
The happiest youth, viewing his progress through,
What perils past, what crosses to ensue,
Would shut the book, and sit him down and die.
'Tis not ten years gone
Since Richard and Northumberland, great friends,
Did feast together, and in two years after
Were they at wars. It is but eight years since
This Percy was the man nearest my soul,
Who like a brother toiled in my affairs
And laid his love and life under my foot,
Yea, for my sake, even to the eyes of Richard
Gave him defiance. But which of you was by—
[*To Warwick*] You, cousin Nevil, as I may remember—
When Richard, with his eye brimful of tears,
Then checked and rated by Northumberland,
Did speak these words, now proved a prophecy:
"Northumberland, thou ladder by the which
My cousin Bolingbroke ascends my throne"—

Though then, God knows, I had no such intent,
But that necessity so bowed the state
That I and greatness were compelled to kiss—
"The time shall come," thus did he follow it,
"The time will come that foul sin, gathering head,
Shall break into corruption." So went on,
Foretelling this same time's condition
And the division of our amity.

Warwick. There is a history in all men's lives,
Figuring the nature of the times deceased,
The which observed, a man may prophesy,
With a near aim, of the main chance of things
As yet not come to life, who in their seeds
And weak beginning lie intreasured.
Such things become the hatch and brood of time,
And by the necessary form of this
King Richard might create a perfect guess
That great Northumberland, then false to him,
Would of that seed grow to a greater falseness,
Which should not find a ground to root upon,
Unless on you.

King.   Are these things then necessities?
Then let us meet them like necessities.
And that same word even now cries out on us.
They say the Bishop and Northumberland
Are fifty thousand strong.

Warwick.   It cannot be, my lord.
Rumor doth double, like the voice and echo,
The numbers of the feared. Please it your Grace
To go to bed. Upon my soul, my lord,
The powers that you already have sent forth
Shall bring this prize in very easily.
To comfort you the more, I have received
A certain instance that Glendower is dead.
Your Majesty hath been this fortnight ill,
And these unseasoned hours perforce must add
Unto your sickness.

King.   I will take your counsel.
And were these inward wars once out of hand,
We would, dear lords, unto the Holy Land.

    [Exeunt]

*[Enter Justice Shallow and Justice Silence
with Moldy, Shadow, Wart, Feeble, Bullcalf]*

Shallow. Come on, come on, come on. Give me your hand, sir, give me your hand, sir; an early stirrer, by the rood! And how doth my good cousin Silence?

Silence. Good morrow, good cousin Shallow.

Shallow. And how doth my cousin, your bedfellow? And your fairest daughter and mine, my goddaughter Ellen?

Silence. Alas, a black ousel, cousin Shallow!

Shallow. By yea and no, sir, I dare say my cousin William is become a good scholar. He is at Oxford still, is he not?

Silence. Indeed, sir, to my cost.

Shallow. 'A must, then, to the Inns o' Court shortly. I was once of Clement's Inn, where I think they will talk of mad Shallow yet.

Silence. You were called "lusty Shallow" then, cousin.

Shallow. By the mass, I was called anything. And I would have done anything indeed too, and roundly too. There was I, and little John Doit of Staffordshire, and black George Barnes, and Francis Pickbone, and Will Squele, a Cotswold man; you had not four such swinge-bucklers in all the Inns o' Court again. And I may say to you we knew where the bona-robas were and had the best of them all at commandment. Then was Jack Falstaff, now Sir John, a boy, and page to Thomas Mowbray, Duke of Norfolk.

Silence. This Sir John, cousin, that comes hither anon about soldiers?

Shallow.	The same Sir John, the very same. I see him break Scoggin's head at the court-gate, when 'a was a crack not thus high. And the very same day did I fight with one Sampson Stockfish, a fruiterer, behind Gray's Inn. Jesu, Jesu, the mad days that I have spent! And to see how many of my old acquaintance are dead!
Silence.	We shall all follow, cousin.
Shallow.	Certain, 'tis certain, very sure, very sure. Death, as the Psalmist saith, is certain to all, all shall die. How a good yoke of bullocks at Stamford Fair?
Silence.	By my troth, I was not there.
Shallow.	Death is certain. Is old Double of your town living yet?
Silence.	Dead, sir.
Shallow.	Jesu, Jesu, dead! 'A drew a good bow, and dead! 'A shot a fine shoot. John a Gaunt loved him well and betted much money on his head. Dead! 'A would have clapped i' th' clout at twelve score, and carried you a forehand shaft a fourteen and fourteen and a half, that it would have done a man's heart good to see. How a score of ewes now?
Silence.	Thereafter as they be. A score of good ewes may be worth ten pounds.
Shallow.	And is old Double dead?
Silence.	Here come two of Sir John Falstaff's men, as I think.
	[*Enter Bardolph and one with him*]
	Good morrow, honest gentlemen.
Bardolph.	I beseech you, which is Justice Shallow?
Shallow.	I am Robert Shallow, sir, a poor esquire of this county, and one of the King's justices of the peace. What is your good pleasure with me?
Bardolph.	My captain, sir, commends him to you, my captain, Sir John Falstaff, a tall gentleman, by heaven, and a most gallant leader.
Shallow.	He greets me well, sir. I knew him a good backsword man. How doth the good knight? May I ask how my lady his wife doth?

Bardolph.	Sir, pardon, a soldier is better accommodated than with a wife.
Shallow.	It is well said, in faith, sir, and it is well said indeed too. "Better accommodated"! It is good, yea, indeed, is it. Good phrases are surely, and ever were, very commendable. "Accommodated"! It comes of *"accommodo."* Very good, a good phrase.
Bardolph.	Pardon, sir. I have heard the word. "Phrase" call you it? By this good day, I know not the phrase, but I will maintain the word with my sword to be a soldier-like word, and a word of exceeding good command, by heaven. "Accommodated," that is, when a man is, as they say, accommodated; or when a man is, being, whereby 'a may be thought to be accommodated, which is an excellent thing.
	[*Enter Falstaff*]
Shallow.	It is very just. Look, here comes good Sir John. Give me your good hand, give me your worship's good hand. By my troth, you like well and bear your years very well. Welcome, good Sir John.
Falstaff.	I am glad to see you well, good Master Robert Shallow. Master Surecard, as I think?
Shallow.	No, Sir John, it is my cousin Silence, in commission with me.
Falstaff.	Good Master Silence, it well befits you should be of the peace.
Silence.	Your good worship is welcome.
Falstaff.	Fie! This is hot weather, gentlemen. Have you provided me here half a dozen sufficient men?
Shallow.	Marry, have we, sir. Will you sit?
Falstaff.	Let me see them, I beseech you.

Shallow.	Where's the roll? Where's the roll? Where's the roll? Let me see, let me see, let me see. So, so, so, so, so, so—so. Yea, marry, sir. Rafe Moldy! Let them appear as I call, let them do so, let them do so. Let me see, where is Moldy?
Moldy.	Here, and't please you.
Shallow.	What think you, Sir John? A good-limbed fellow, young, strong, and of good friends.
Falstaff.	Is thy name Moldy?
Moldy.	Yea, and't please you.
Falstaff.	'Tis the more time thou wert used.
Shallow.	Ha, ha, ha! Most excellent, i' faith! Things that are moldy lack use. Very singular good! In faith, well said, Sir John, very well said.
Falstaff.	Prick him.
Moldy.	I was pricked well enough before, and you could have let me alone. My old dame will be undone now for one to do her husbandry and her drudgery. You need not to have pricked me. There are other men fitter to go out than I.
Falstaff.	Go to. Peace, Moldy, you shall go. Moldy, it is time you were spent.
Moldy.	Spent?
Shallow.	Peace, fellow, peace. Stand aside. Know you where you are? For th' other, Sir John, let me see. Simon Shadow!
Falstaff.	Yea, marry, let me have him to sit under. He's like to be a cold soldier.
Shallow.	Where's Shadow?
Shadow.	Here, sir.
Falstaff.	Shadow, whose son art thou?
Shadow.	My mother's son, sir.
Falstaff.	Thy mother's son! Like enough, and thy father's shadow. So the son of the female is the shadow of the male. It is often so, indeed, but much of the father's substance!

Shallow.	Do you like him, Sir John?
Falstaff.	Shadow will serve for summer. Prick him, for we have a number of shadows fill up the musterbook.
Shallow.	Thomas Wart!
Falstaff.	Where's he?
Wart.	Here, sir.
Falstaff.	Is thy name Wart?
Wart.	Yea, sir.
Falstaff.	Thou art a very ragged wart.
Shallow.	Shall I prick him, Sir John?
Falstaff.	It were superfluous, for his apparel is built upon his back and the whole frame stands upon pins. Prick him no more.
Shallow.	Ha, ha, ha! You can do it, sir! You can do it! I commend you well. Francis Feeble!
Feeble.	Here, sir.
Shallow.	What trade art thou, Feeble?
Feeble.	A woman's tailor, sir.
Shallow.	Shall I prick him, sir?
Falstaff.	You may. But if he had been a man's tailor, he'd a' pricked you. Wilt thou make as many holes in an enemy's battle as thou hast done in a woman's petticoat?
Feeble.	I will do my good will, sir. You can have no more.
Falstaff.	Well said, good woman's tailor! Well said, courageous Feeble! Thou wilt be as valiant as the wrathful dove or most magnanimous mouse. Prick the woman's tailor well, Master Shallow, deep, Master Shallow.
Feeble.	I would Wart might have gone, sir.

Falstaff.	I would thou wert a man's tailor, that thou mightst mend him and make him fit to go. I cannot put him to a private soldier that is the leader of so many thousands. Let that suffice, most forcible Feeble.
Feeble.	It shall suffice, sir.
Falstaff.	I am bound to thee, reverend Feeble. Who is next?
Shallow.	Peter Bullcalf o' th' green!
Falstaff.	Yea, marry, let's see Bullcalf.
Bullcalf.	Here, sir.
Falstaff.	'Fore God, a likely fellow! Come, prick Bullcalf till he roar again.
Bullcalf.	O Lord, good my lord captain—
Falstaff.	What, dost thou roar before thou art pricked?
Bullcalf.	O Lord, sir, I am a diseased man.
Falstaff.	What disease hast thou?
Bullcalf.	A whoreson cold, sir, a cough, sir, which I caught with ringing in the King's affairs upon his coronation day, sir.
Falstaff.	Come, thou shalt go to the wars in a gown. We will have away thy cold, and I will take such order that thy friends shall ring for thee. Is here all?
Shallow.	Here is two more called than your number. You must have but four here, sir. And so, I pray you, go in with me to dinner.
Falstaff.	Come, I will go drink with you, but I cannot tarry dinner. I am glad to see you, by my troth, Master Shallow.
Shallow.	O, Sir John, do you remember since we lay all night in the Windmill in Saint George's Field?
Falstaff.	No more of that, Master Shallow.
Shallow.	Ha! 'Twas a merry night. And is Jane Nightwork alive?
Falstaff.	She lives, Master Shallow.
Shallow.	She never could away with me.

Falstaff.	Never, never, she would always say she could not abide Master Shallow.
Shallow.	By the mass, I could anger her to th' heart. She was then a bona-roba. Doth she hold her own well?
Falstaff.	Old, old, Master Shallow.
Shallow.	Nay, she must be old. She cannot choose but be old. Certain she's old, and had Robin Nightwork by old Nightwork before I came to Clement's Inn.
Silence.	That's fifty-five year ago.
Shallow.	Ha, cousin Silence, that thou hadst seen that this knight and I have seen! Ha, Sir John, said I well?
Falstaff.	We have heard the chimes at midnight, Master Shallow.
Shallow.	That we have, that we have, that we have, in faith, Sir John, we have. Our watchword was "Hem, boys!" Come, let's to dinner, come, let's to dinner. Jesus, the days that we have seen! Come, come.
	[Exeunt Falstaff and the Justices]
Bullcalf.	Good Master Corporate Bardolph, stand my friend, and here's four Harry ten shillings in French crowns for you. In very truth, sir, I had as lief be hanged, sir, as go. And yet for mine own part, sir, I do not care, but rather, because I am unwilling, and, for mine own part, have a desire to stay with my friends. Else, sir, I did not care, for mine own part, so much.
Bardolph.	Go to, stand aside.
Moldy.	And, good Master Corporal Captain, for my dame's sake, stand my friend. She has nobody to do anything about her when I am gone, and she is old and cannot help herself. You shall have forty, sir.
Bardolph.	Go to, stand aside.

Feeble.	By my troth, I care not. A man can die but once. We owe God a death. I'll ne'er bear a base mind. And't be my destiny, so. And't be not, so. No man's too good to serve's Prince. And let it go which way it will, he that dies this year is quit for the next.
Bardolph.	Well said. Th' art a good fellow.
Feeble.	Faith, I'll bear no base mind.
	[Enter Falstaff and the Justices]
Falstaff.	Come, sir, which men shall I have?
Shallow.	Four of which you please.
Bardolph.	Sir, a word with you. *[Aside]* I have three pound to free Moldy and Bullcalf.
Falstaff.	Go to, well.
Shallow.	Come, Sir John, which four will you have?
Falstaff.	Do you choose for me.
Shallow.	Marry, then, Moldy, Bullcalf, Feeble, and Shadow.
Falstaff.	Moldy and Bullcalf. For you, Moldy, stay at home till you are past service. And for your part, Bullcalf, grow till you come unto it. I will none of you.
Shallow.	Sir John, Sir John, do not yourself wrong. They are your likeliest men, and I would have you served with the best.
Falstaff.	Will you tell me, Master Shallow, how to choose a man? Care I for the limb, the thews, the stature, bulk, and big assemblance of a man? Give me the spirit, Master Shallow! Here's Wart. You see what a ragged appearance it is. 'A shall charge you and discharge you with the motion of a pewterer's hammer, come off and on swifter than he that gibbets on the brewer's bucket. And this same half-faced fellow, Shadow. Give me this man. He presents no mark to the enemy: the foeman may with as great aim level at the edge of a penknife. And for a retreat, how swiftly will this Feeble the woman's tailor run off! O, give me the spare men, and spare me the great ones. Put me a caliver into Wart's hand, Bardolph.

Bardolph.	Hold, Wart, traverse. Thus, thus, thus.
Falstaff.	Come, manage me your caliver. So. Very well. Go to. Very good, exceeding good. O, give me always a little, lean, old, chopped bald shot. Well said, i' faith, Wart. Th' art a good scab. Hold, there's a tester for thee.
Shallow.	He is not his craft's master, he doth not do it right. I remember at Mile-End Green, when I lay at Clement's Inn—I was then Sir Dagonet in Arthur's show— there was a little quiver fellow, and 'a would manage you his piece thus, and 'a would about and about, and come you in and come you in. "Rah, tah, tah," would 'a say, "Bounce," would 'a say, and away again would 'a go, and again would 'a come. I shall ne'er see such a fellow.
Falstaff.	These fellows would do well, Master Shallow. God keep you, Master Silence. I will not use many words with you. Fare you well, gentlemen both. I thank you. I must a dozen mile tonight. Bardolph, give the soldiers coats.
Shallow.	Sir John, the Lord bless you! God prosper your affairs! God send us peace! At your return visit our house, let our old acquaintance be renewed. Peradventure I will with ye to the court.
Falstaff.	'Fore God, would you would.
Shallow.	Go to, I have spoke at a word. God keep you.

Falstaff.   Fare you well, gentle gentlemen. [*Exeunt Justices*] On, Bardolph, lead the men away. [*Exeunt all but Falstaff*] As I return, I will fetch off these justices. I do see the bottom of Justice Shallow. Lord, Lord, how subject we old men are to this vice of lying! This same starved justice hath done nothing but prate to me of the wildness of his youth and the feats he hath done about Turnbull Street, and every third word a lie, duer paid to the hearer than the Turk's tribute. I do remember him at Clement's Inn like a man made after supper of a cheese-paring. When 'a was naked, he was, for all the world, like a forked radish, with a head fantastically carved upon it with a knife. 'A was so forlorn that his dimensions to any thick sight were invisible. 'A was the very genius of famine, yet lecherous as a monkey, and the whores called him mandrake. 'A came ever in the rearward of the fashion, and sung those tunes to the overscutched huswives that he heard the carmen whistle, and sware they were his fancies or his goodnights. And now is this Vice's dagger become a squire, and talks as familiarly of John a Gaunt as if he had been sworn brother to him, and I'll be sworn 'a ne'er saw him but once in the Tilt-yard, and then he burst his head for crowding among the marshal's men. I saw it, and told John a Gaunt he beat his own name, for you might have thrust him and all his apparel into an eel-skin—the case of a treble hautboy was a mansion for him, a court. And now has he land and beeves. Well, I'll be acquainted with him, if I return, and 't shall go hard but I'll make him a philosopher's two stones to me. If the young dace be a bait for the old pike, I see no reason in the law of nature but I may snap at him. Let time shape, and there an end.

     [*Exit*]

PART II ACT FOUR

WITH THE REBEL ARMY

[Enter the Archbishop of York, with Mowbray,
Hastings and others within Gaultree Forest]

Archbishop. What is this forest called?

Hastings. 'Tis Gaultree Forest, and't shall please your Grace.

Archbishop. Here stand, my lords, and send discoverers forth
To know the numbers of our enemies.

Hastings. We have sent forth already.

Archbishop.   'Tis well done.
My friends and brethren in these great affairs,
I must acquaint you that I have received
New-dated letters from Northumberland,
Their cold intent, tenor, and substance, thus:
Here doth he wish his person, with such powers
As might hold sortance with his quality,
The which he could not levy. Whereupon
He is retired, to ripe his growing fortunes,
To Scotland, and concludes in hearty prayers
That your attempts may overlive the hazard
And fearful meeting of their opposite.

Mowbray. Thus do the hopes we have in him touch ground
And dash themselves to pieces.

[Enter Messenger]

Hastings.	Now, what news?
Messenger.	West of this forest, scarcely off a mile,
	In goodly form comes on the enemy,
	And, by the ground they hide, I judge their number
	Upon or near the rate of thirty thousand.
Mowbray.	The just proportion that we gave them out:
	Let us sway on and face them in the field.
Archbishop.	What well-appointed leader fronts us here?
	[Enter Westmoreland]
Mowbray.	I think it is my Lord of Westmoreland.
Westmoreland.	Health and fair greeting from our general,
	The Prince, Lord John and Duke of Lancaster.
Archbishop.	Say on, my Lord of Westmoreland, in peace.
	What doth concern your coming?

Westmoreland.   Then, my lord,
          Unto your Grace do I in chief address
          The substance of my speech. If that rebellion
          Came like itself, in base and abject routs,
          Led on by bloody youth, guarded with rage,
          And countenanced by boys and beggary,
          I say, if damned commotion so appeared,
          In his true, native and most proper shape,
          You, reverend father, and these noble lords
          Had not been here, to dress the ugly form
          Of base and bloody insurrection
          With your fair honors. You, Lord Archbishop,
          Whose see is by a civil peace maintained,
          Whose beard the silver hand of peace hath touched,
          Whose learning and good letters peace hath tutored,
          Whose white investments figure innocence,
          The dove and very blessed spirit of peace,
          Wherefore do you so ill translate yourself
          Out of the speech of peace that bears such grace,
          Into the harsh and boisterous tongue of war,
          Turning your books to graves, your ink to blood,
          Your pens to lances, and your tongue divine
          To a loud trumpet and a point of war?

Archbishop. Wherefore do I this? So the question stands.
Briefly to this end: we are all diseased,
And with our surfeiting and wanton hours
Have brought ourselves into a burning fever,
And we must bleed for it. Of which disease
Our late king, Richard, being infected, died.
But, my most noble Lord of Westmoreland,
I take not on me here as a physician,
Nor do I as an enemy to peace
Troop in the throngs of military men,
But rather show awhile like fearful war,
To diet rank minds sick of happiness
And purge th' obstructions which begin to stop
Our very veins of life. Hear me more plainly.
I have in equal balance justly weighed
What wrongs our arms may do, what wrongs we suffer,
And find our griefs heavier than our offenses.
We see which way the stream of time doth run,
And are enforced from our most quiet there
By the rough torrent of occasion,
And have the summary of all our griefs,
When time shall serve, to show in articles;
Which long ere this we offered to the King,
And might by no suit gain our audience.
When we are wronged and would unfold our griefs,
We are denied access unto his person

Even by those men that most have done us wrong.
The dangers of the days but newly gone,
Whose memory is written on the earth
With yet-appearing blood, and the examples
Of every minute's instance, present now,
Hath put us in these ill-beseeming arms,
Not to break peace or any branch of it,
But to establish here a peace indeed,
Concurring both in name and quality.

Westmoreland. When ever yet was your appeal denied?
Wherein have you been galled by the King?
What peer hath been suborned to grate on you,
That you should seal this lawless bloody book
Of forged rebellion with a seal divine?

Archbishop. My brother general, the commonwealth,
I make my quarrel in particular.

Westmoreland. There is no need of any such redress,
Or if there were, it not belongs to you.

Mowbray. Why not to him in part, and to us all
That feel the bruises of the days before,
And suffer the condition of these times
To lay a heavy and unequal hand
Upon our honors?

Westmoreland.   O, my good Lord Mowbray,
Construe the times to their necessities,
And you shall say indeed, it is the time,
And not the King, that doth you injuries.
Yet for your part, it not appears to me
Either from the King or in the present time
That you should have an inch of any ground
To build a grief on. Were you not restored
To all the Duke of Norfolk's signories,
Your noble and right well-rememb'red father's?

Mowbray.   What thing, in honor, had my father lost,
That need to be revived and breathed in me?
The King that loved him, as the state stood then,
Was force perforce compelled to banish him.
And then that Henry Bolingbroke and he,
Being mounted and both roused in their seats,
Their neighing coursers daring of the spur,
Their armed staves in charge, their beavers down,
Their eyes of fire sparkling through sights of steel,
And the loud trumpet blowing them together,
Then, then, when there was nothing could have stayed
My father from the breast of Bolingbroke —
O, when the King did throw his warder down
His own life hung upon the staff he threw.
Then threw he down himself and all their lives
That by indictment and by dint of sword
Have since miscarried under Bolingbroke.

Westmoreland. You speak, Lord Mowbray, now you know not what.
The Earl of Hereford was reputed then
In England the most valiant gentleman.
Who knows on whom Fortune would then have smiled?
But if your father had been victor there,
He ne'er had borne it out of Coventry.
For all the country in a general voice
Cried hate upon him, and all their prayers and love
Were set on Hereford, whom they doted on
And blessed and graced—and did more than the King.
But this is mere digression from my purpose.
Here come I from our princely general
To know your griefs, to tell you from his Grace
That he will give you audience, and wherein
It shall appear that your demands are just,
You shall enjoy them, everything set off
That might so much as think you enemies.

Mowbray. But he hath forced us to compel this offer,
And it proceeds from policy, not love.

Westmoreland.	Mowbray, you overween to take it so.
	This offer comes from mercy, not from fear.
	For, lo, within a ken our army lies,
	Upon mine honor, all too confident
	To give admittance to a thought of fear.
	Our battle is more full of names than yours,
	Our men more perfect in the use of arms,
	Our armor all as strong, our cause the best.
	Then reason will our hearts should be as good.
	Say you not then our offer is compelled.
Mowbray.	Well, by my will we shall admit no parley.
Westmoreland.	That argues but the shame of your offense.
	A rotten case abides no handling.
Hastings.	Hath the Prince John a full commission,
	In very ample virtue of his father,
	To hear and absolutely to determine
	Of what conditions we shall stand upon?
Westmoreland.	That is intended in the General's name.
	I muse you make so slight a question.

Archbishop.	Then take, my Lord of Westmoreland, this schedule,
	For this contains our general grievances.
	Each several article herein redressed,
	All members of our cause, both here and hence
	That are insinewed to this action,
	Acquitted by a true substantial form
	And present execution of our wills
	To us and our purposes confined,
	We come within our awful banks again
	And knit our powers to the arm of peace.
Westmoreland.	This will I show the General. Please you, lords,
	In sight of both our battles we may meet,
	And either end in peace—which God so frame—
	Or to the place of diff'rence call the swords
	Which must decide it.
Archbishop.	My lord, we will do so.

[Exit Westmoreland]

Mowbray.	There is a thing within my bosom tells me
	That no conditions of our peace can stand.
Hastings.	Fear you not that. If we can make our peace
	Upon such large terms and so absolute
	As our conditions shall consist upon,
	Our peace shall stand as firm as rocky mountains.

Mowbray.	Yea, but our valuation shall be such
	That every slight and false-derived cause,
	Yea, every idle, nice, and wanton reason
	Shall to the King taste of this action,
	That, were our royal faiths martyrs in love,
	We shall be winnowed with so rough a wind
	That even our corn shall seem as light as chaff
	And good from bad find no partition.
Archbishop.	No, no, my lord. Note this. The King is weary
	Of dainty and such picking grievances.
	For he hath found to end one doubt by death
	Revives two greater in the heirs of life,
	And therefore will he wipe his tables clean
	And keep no telltale to his memory
	That may repeat and history his loss
	To new remembrance. For full well he knows
	He cannot so precisely weed this land
	As his misdoubts present occasion.
	His foes are so enrooted with his friends
	That, plucking to unfix an enemy,
	He doth unfasten so and shake a friend.
	So that this land, like an offensive wife
	That hath enraged him on to offer strokes,
	As he is striking, holds his infant up
	And hangs resolved correction in the arm
	That was upreared to execution.

Hastings.	Besides, the King hath wasted all his rods
	On late offenders, that he now doth lack
	The very instruments of chastisement.
	So that his power, like to a fangless lion,
	May offer, but not hold.
Archbishop.	'Tis very true.
	And therefore be assured, my good Lord Marshal,
	If we do now make our atonement well,
	Our peace will, like a broken limb united,
	Grow stronger for the breaking.
Mowbray.	Be it so.
	Here is returned my Lord of Westmoreland.

[Enter Westmoreland]

Westmoreland.	The Prince is here at hand. Pleaseth your lordship
	To meet his Grace just distance 'tween our armies.

[Enter Prince John of Lancaster and his army]

Mowbray.	Your Grace of York, in God's name then, set forward.
Archbishop.	Before, and greet his Grace, my lord; we come.
Lancaster.	You are well encount'red here, my cousin Mowbray.
	Good day to you, gentle Lord Archbishop.
	And so to you, Lord Hastings, and to all.
	My Lord of York, it better showed with you
	When that your flock, assembled by the bell,
	Encircled you to hear with reverence

Your exposition on the holy text
Than now to see you here an iron man talking,
Cheering a rout of rebels with your drum,
Turning the word to sword and life to death.
That man that sits within a monarch's heart
And ripens in the sunshine of his favor,
Would he abuse the countenance of the King,
Alack, what mischiefs might he set abroach
In shadow of such greatness! With you, Lord Bishop,
It is even so. Who hath not heard it spoken
How deep you were within the books of God?
To us the speaker in His parliament,
To us th' imagined voice of God himself,
The very opener and intelligencer
Between the grace, the sanctities of heaven
And our dull workings. O, who shall believe
But you misuse the reverence of your place,
Employ the countenance and grace of heaven,
As a false favorite doth his prince's name,
In deeds dishonorable? You have ta'en up,
Under the counterfeited zeal of God,
The subjects of His substitute, my father,
And both against the peace of heaven and him
Have here upswarmed them.

Archbishop.   Good my Lord of Lancaster,
           I am not here against your father's peace,
           But, as I told my Lord of Westmoreland,
           The time misord'red doth, in common sense,
           Crowd us and crush us to this monstrous form,
           To hold our safety up. I sent your Grace
           The parcels and particulars of our grief,
           The which hath been with scorn shoved from the court,
           Whereon this Hydra son of war is born,
           Whose dangerous eyes may well be charmed asleep
           With grant of our most just and right desires,
           And true obedience, of this madness cured,
           Stoop tamely to the foot of majesty.
Mowbray. If not, we ready are to try our fortunes
           To the last man.
Hastings.   And though we here fall down,
           We have supplies to second our attempt.
           If they miscarry, theirs shall second them,
           And so success of mischief shall be born
           And heir from heir shall hold this quarrel up
           Whiles England shall have generation.
Lancaster. You are too shallow, Hastings, much too shallow,
           To sound the bottom of the after-times.
Westmoreland. Pleaseth your Grace to answer them directly
           How far forth you do like their articles.

Lancaster.	I like them all, and do allow them well,
	And swear here, by the honor of my blood,
	My father's purposes have been mistook,
	And some about him have too lavishly
	Wrested his meaning and authority.
	My lord, these griefs shall be with speed redressed.
	Upon my soul, they shall. If this may please you,
	Discharge your powers unto their several counties,
	As we will ours. And here between the armies
	Let's drink together friendly and embrace,
	That all their eyes may bear those tokens home
	Of our restored love and amity.
Archbishop.	I take your princely word for these redresses.
Lancaster.	I give it you, and will maintain my word.
	And thereupon I drink unto your Grace. [*He drinks*]
Hastings.	Go, Captain, and deliver to the army
	This news of peace. Let them have pay, and part.
	I know it will well please them. Hie thee, Captain.
	[*Exit Officer*]
Archbishop.	To you, my noble Lord of Westmoreland. [*He drinks*]
Westmoreland.	I pledge your Grace, and, if you knew what pains
	I have bestowed to breed this present peace,
	You would drink freely. But my love to ye
	Shall show itself more openly hereafter.

Archbishop.	I do not doubt you.
Westmoreland.	I am glad of it.
	Health to my lord and gentle cousin, Mowbray.
Mowbray.	You wish me health in very happy season,
	For I am, on the sudden, something ill.
Archbishop.	Against ill chances men are ever merry,
	But heaviness foreruns the good event.
Westmoreland.	Therefore be merry, coz, since sudden sorrow
	Serves to say thus, "Some good thing comes tomorrow."
Archbishop.	Believe me, I am passing light in spirit.
Mowbray.	So much the worse, if your own rule be true.

    [*Shout within*]

Lancaster.	The word of peace is rend'red. Hark, how they shout!
Mowbray.	This had been cheerful after victory.
Archbishop.	A peace is of the nature of a conquest,
	For then both parties nobly are subdued,
	And neither party loser.
Lancaster.	Go, my lord,
	And let our army be discharged too.

    [*Exit Westmoreland*]

  And, good my lord, so please you, let our trains
  March by us, that we may peruse the men
  We should have coped withal.

Archbishop.   Go, good Lord Hastings,
          And, ere they be dismissed, let them march by.
                    [Exit Hastings]
Lancaster.   I trust, lords, we shall lie tonight together.
                    [Enter Westmoreland]
          Now cousin, wherefore stands our army still?
Westmoreland.   The leaders, having charge from you to stand,
          Will not go off until they hear you speak.
Lancaster.   They know their duties.
                    [Enter Hastings]
Hastings.   My lord, our army is dispersed already.
          Like youthful steers unyoked, they take their courses
          East, west, north, south, or, like a school broke up,
          Each hurries toward his home and sporting-place.
Westmoreland.   Good tidings, my Lord Hastings, for the which
          I do arrest thee, traitor, of high treason.
          And you, Lord Archbishop, and you, Lord Mowbray,
          Of capital treason I attach you both.
Mowbray.   Is this proceeding just and honorable?
Westmoreland.   Is your assembly so?
Archbishop.   [To Prince John] Will you thus break your faith?

Lancaster.   I pawned thee none.
I promised you redress of these same grievances
Whereof you did complain, which, by mine honor,
I will perform with a most Christian care.
But for you, rebels, look to taste the due
Meet for rebellion and such acts as yours.
Most shallowly did you these arms commence,
Fondly brought here and foolishly sent hence.
Strike up our drums, pursue the scatt'red stray.
God, and not we, hath safely fought today.
Some guard these traitors to the block of death,
Treason's true bed and yielder up of breath.
     [*Exeunt*]

[Alarum. Enter Falstaff and Coleville, meeting. Excursions]

Falstaff. What's your name, sir? Of what condition are you, and of what place?

Coleville. I am a knight, sir, and my name is Coleville of the Dale.

Falstaff. Well, then, Coleville is your name, a knight is your degree, and your place the Dale. Coleville shall be still your name, a traitor your degree, and the dungeon your place, a place deep enough. So shall you be still Coleville of the Dale.

Coleville. Are not you Sir John Falstaff?

Falstaff. As good a man as he, sir, whoe'er I am. Do ye yield, sir, or shall I sweat for you? If I do sweat, they are the drops of thy lovers, and they weep for thy death. Therefore rouse up fear and trembling, and do observance to my mercy.

Coleville. I think you are Sir John Falstaff, and in that thought yield me.

Falstaff. I have a whole school of tongues in this belly of mine, and not a tongue of them all speaks any other word but my name. And I had but a belly of any indifferency, I were simply the most active fellow in Europe. My womb, my womb, my womb undoes me. Here comes our general.

*[Enter Prince John of Lancaster, Westmore-
land, Blunt, and the rest. Retreat sounded]*

Lancaster. The heat is past, follow no further now.
Call in the powers, good cousin Westmoreland.

[Exit Westmoreland]

Now, Falstaff, where have you been all this while?
When everything is ended, then you come.
These tardy tricks of yours will, on my life,
One time or other break some gallows' back.

Falstaff. I would be sorry, my lord, but it should be thus. I never knew yet but rebuke and check was the reward of valor. Do you think me a swallow, an arrow, or a bullet? Have I, in my poor and old motion, the expedition of thought? I have speeded hither with the very extremest inch of possibility. I have found'red nine score and odd posts, and here, travel-tainted as I am, have, in my pure and immaculate valor, taken Sir John Coleville of the Dale, a most furious knight and valorous enemy. But what of that? He saw me, and yielded, that I may justly say, with the hook-nosed fellow of Rome, "There, cousin, I came, saw, and overcame."

Lancaster. It was more of his courtesy than your deserving.

Falstaff. I know not. Here he is, and here I yield him. And I beseech your Grace, let it be booked with the rest of this day's deeds, or, by the Lord, I will have it in a particular ballad else, with mine own picture on the top on't, Coleville kissing my foot. To the which course if I be enforced, if you do not all show like gilt twopences to me, and I in the clear sky of fame o'ershine you as much as the full moon doth the cinders of the element, which show like pins' heads to her, believe not the word of the noble. Therefore let me have right, and let desert mount.

Lancaster. Thine's too heavy to mount.

Falstaff. Let it shine, then.

Lancaster. Thine's too thick to shine.

Falstaff. Let it do something, my good lord, that may do me good, and call it what you will.

Lancaster. Is thy name Coleville?

Coleville. It is, my lord.

Lancaster. A famous rebel art thou, Coleville.

Falstaff. And a famous true subject took him.

Coleville.   I am, my lord, but as my betters are
                    That led me hither. Had they been ruled by me,
                    You should have won them dearer than you have.

Falstaff.	I know not how they sold themselves. But thou, like a kind fellow, gavest thyself away gratis, and I thank thee for thee.

[Enter Westmoreland]

Lancaster.	Now, have you left pursuit?
Westmoreland.	Retreat is made and execution stayed.
Lancaster.	Send Coleville with his confederates
	To York, to present execution.
	Blunt, lead him hence, and see you guard him sure.

[Exeunt Blunt and others with Coleville]

And now dispatch we toward the court, my lords.

I hear the King my father is sore sick.

Our news shall go before us to his Majesty,

Which, cousin, you shall bear to comfort him,

And we with sober speed will follow you.

Falstaff.	My lord, I beseech you give me leave to go
	Through Gloucestershire. And when you come to court,
	Stand my good lord in your good report.
Lancaster.	Fare you well, Falstaff. I, in my condition,
	Shall better speak of you than you deserve.

[Exeunt all but Falstaff]

Falstaff.	I would you had the wit. 'Twere better than your dukedom. Good faith, this same young sober-blooded boy doth not love me, nor a man cannot make him laugh. But that's no marvel, he drinks no wine. There's never none of these demure boys come to any proof, for thin drink doth so overcool their blood, and making many fish-meals, that they fall into a kind of male green-sickness, and then, when they marry, they get wenches. They are generally fools and cowards, which some of us should be too, but for inflammation. A good sherris-sack hath

a twofold operation in it. It ascends me into the brain, dries me there all the foolish and dull and cruddy vapors which environ it, makes it apprehensive, quick, forgetive, full of nimble, fiery, and delectable shapes, which, delivered o'er to the voice, the tongue, which is the birth, becomes excellent wit. The second property of your excellent sherris is the warming of the blood, which, before cold and settled, left the liver white and pale, which is the badge of pusillanimity and cowardice. But the sherris warms it and makes it course from the inwards to the parts extremes. It illumineth the face, which as a beacon gives warning to all the rest of this little kingdom, man, to arm, and then the vital commoners and inland petty spirits muster me all to their captain, the heart, who, great and puffed up with this retinue, doth any deed of courage, and this valor comes of sherris. So that skill in the weapon is nothing without sack, for that sets it a-work, and learning a mere hoard of gold kept by a devil, till sack commences it and sets it in act and use. Hereof comes it that Prince Harry is valiant, for the cold blood he did naturally inherit of his father, he hath, like lean, sterile, and bare land, manured, husbanded, and tilled with excellent endeavor of drinking good and good store of fertile sherris, that he is become very hot and valiant. If I had a thousand sons, the first humane principle I would teach them should be to forswear thin potations and to addict themselves to sack.

       [Enter Bardolph]

How now, Bardolph?

Bardolph. The army is discharged all and gone.

Falstaff. Let them go. I'll through Gloucestershire, and there will I visit Master Robert Shallow, Esquire. I have him already temp'ring between my finger and my thumb, and shortly will I seal with him. Come away.

       [Exeunt]

*[Enter the King, Warwick, Kent, Thomas, the Duke of
Clarence, Humphrey, Duke of Gloucester, and others]*

King.   Now, lords, if God doth give successful end
To this debate that bleedeth at our doors,
We will our youth lead on to higher fields
And draw no swords but what are sanctified.
Our navy is addressed, our power collected,
Our substitutes in absence well invested,
And everything lies level to our wish.
Only, we want a little personal strength
And pause us, till these rebels, now afoot,
Come underneath the yoke of government.

Warwick.   Both which we doubt not but your Majesty
Shall soon enjoy.

King.   Humphrey, my son of Gloucester,
Where is the Prince your brother?

Gloucester.   I think he's gone to hunt, my lord, at Windsor.

King.   And how accompanied?

Gloucester.   I do not know, my lord.

King.   Is not his brother, Thomas of Clarence, with him?

Gloucester.   No, my good lord, he is in presence here.

Clarence.   What would my lord and father?

King.   Nothing but well to thee, Thomas of Clarence.
How chance thou art not with the Prince thy brother?
He loves thee, and thou dost neglect him, Thomas;
Thou hast a better place in his affection
Than all thy brothers. Cherish it, my boy,
And noble offices thou mayst effect
Of mediation, after I am dead,
Between his greatness and thy other brethren.
Therefore omit him not, blunt not his love,
Nor lose the good advantage of his grace
By seeming cold or careless of his will.
For he is gracious, if he be observed.
He hath a tear for pity and a hand
Open as day for meeting charity.
Yet notwithstanding, being incensed, he's flint,
As humorous as winter and as sudden
As flaws congealed in the spring of day.
His temper, therefore, must be well observed.
Chide him for faults, and do it reverently,
When you perceive his blood inclined to mirth,
But, being moody, give him time and scope,
Till that his passions, like a whale on ground,
Confound themselves with working. Learn this, Thomas,
And thou shalt prove a shelter to thy friends,
A hoop of gold to bind thy brothers in,

That the united vessel of their blood,
Mingled with venom of suggestion —
As, force perforce, the age will pour it in —
Shall never leak, though it do work as strong
As aconitum or rash gunpowder.

Clarence. I shall observe him with all care and love.

King. Why art thou not at Windsor with him, Thomas?

Clarence. He is not there today. He dines in London.

King. And how accompanied? Canst thou tell that?

Clarence. With Poins and other his continual followers.

King. Most subject is the fattest soil to weeds,
And he, the noble image of my youth,
Is overspread with them. Therefore my grief
Stretches itself beyond the hour of death.
The blood weeps from my heart when I do shape
In forms imaginary th' unguided days
And rotten times that you shall look upon
When I am sleeping with my ancestors.
For when his headstrong riot hath no curb,
When rage and hot blood are his counselors,
When means and lavish manners meet together,
O, with what wings shall his affections fly
Towards fronting peril and opposed decay!

Warwick. My gracious lord, you look beyond him quite.
The Prince but studies his companions
Like a strange tongue, wherein, to gain the language,
'Tis needful that the most immodest word
Be looked upon and learned, which once attained,
Your Highness knows, comes to no further use
But to be known and hated. So, like gross terms,
The Prince will in the perfectness of time
Cast off his followers, and their memory
Shall as a pattern or a measure live,
By which his Grace must mete the lives of others,
Turning past evils to advantages.

King. 'Tis seldom when the bee doth leave her comb
In the dead carrion. Who's here? Westmoreland?

[*Enter Westmoreland*]

Westmoreland. Health to my sovereign, and new happiness
Added to that that I am to deliver.
Prince John your son doth kiss your Grace's hand.
Mowbray, the Bishop Scroop, Hastings and all
Are brought to the correction of your law.
There is not now a rebel's sword unsheathed,
But Peace puts forth her olive everywhere.
The manner how this action hath been borne
Here at more leisure may your Highness read,
With every course in his particular.

King.	O Westmoreland, thou art a summer bird,
	Which ever in the haunch of winter sings
	The lifting up of day.

	Look, here's more news.
Harcourt.	From enemies, heavens keep your Majesty,
	And, when they stand against you, may they fall
	As those that I am come to tell you of!
	The Earl Northumberland and the Lord Bardolph,
	With a great power of English and of Scots,
	Are by the shrieve of Yorkshire overthrown.
	The manner and true order of the fight
	This packet, please it you, contains at large.
King.	And wherefore should these good news make me sick?
	Will Fortune never come with both hands full,
	But write her fair words still in foulest letters?
	She either gives a stomach and no food—
	Such are the poor, in health—or else a feast
	And takes away the stomach—such are the rich
	That have abundance and enjoy it not.
	I should rejoice now at this happy news,
	And now my sight fails, and my brain is giddy.
	O me! Come near me. Now I am much ill.

Gloucester.	Comfort, your Majesty!
Clarence.	O my royal father!
Westmoreland.	My sovereign lord, cheer up yourself, look up.
Warwick.	Be patient, Princes. You do know these fits
	Are with his Highness very ordinary.
	Stand from him, give him air, he'll straight be well.
Clarence.	No, no, he cannot long hold out these pangs.
	Th' incessant care and labor of his mind
	Hath wrought the mure that should confine it in
	So thin that life looks through and will break out.
Gloucester.	The people fear me, for they do observe
	Unfathered heirs and loathly births off nature.
	The seasons change their manners, as the year
	Had found some months asleep and leaped them over.
Clarence.	The river hath thrice flowed, no ebb between,
	And the old folk, time's doting chronicles,
	Say it did so a little time before
	That our great-grandsire, Edward, sicked and died.
Warwick.	Speak lower, Princes, for the King recovers.
Gloucester.	This apoplexy will certain be his end.
King.	I pray you, take me up, and bear me hence
	Into some other chamber. Softly, pray.

[They bear him to another part of the stage]

Let there be no noise made, my gentle friends,
Unless some dull and favorable hand
Will whisper music to my weary spirit.

Warwick.	Call for the music in the other room.
King.	Set me the crown upon my pillow here.
Clarence.	His eye is hollow, and he changes much.
Warwick.	Less noise, less noise!

[*Enter Prince Harry*]

Prince.	Who saw the Duke of Clarence?
Clarence.	I am here, brother, full of heaviness.
Prince.	How now! Rain within doors, and none abroad! How doth the King?
Gloucester.	Exceeding ill.
Prince.	Heard he the good news yet? Tell it him.
Gloucester.	He altered much upon the hearing it.
Prince.	If he be sick with joy, he'll recover without physic.
Warwick.	Not so much noise, my lords. Sweet Prince, speak low. The King your father is disposed to sleep.
Clarence.	Let us withdraw into the other room.
Warwick.	Will't please your Grace to go along with us?
Prince.	No, I will sit and watch here by the King.

[*Exeunt all but Prince Hal*]

Why doth the crown lie there upon his pillow,
Being so troublesome a bedfellow?
O polished perturbation! Golden care!
That keep'st the ports of slumber open wide
To many a watchful night! Sleep with it now!
Yet not so sound and half so deeply sweet
As he whose brow with homely biggen bound
Snores out the watch of night. O majesty!
When thou dost pinch thy bearer, thou dost sit
Like a rich armor worn in heat of day,
That scald'st with safety. By his gates of breath
There lies a downy feather which stirs not.
Did he suspire, that light and weightless down
Perforce must move. My gracious lord, my father!
This sleep is sound indeed. This is a sleep
That from this golden rigol hath divorced
So many English kings. Thy due from me
Is tears and heavy sorrows of the blood,
Which nature, love, and filial tenderness
Shall, O dear father, pay thee plenteously.
My due from thee is this imperial crown,
Which, as immediate from thy place and blood,
Derives itself to me. [*Puts on the crown*] Lo, where it sits,
Which God shall guard. And put the world's whole strength
Into one giant arm, it shall not force
This lineal honor from me. This from thee
Will I to mine leave, as 'tis left to me.

      [*Exit*]

King.	[*Waking*] Warwick! Gloucester! Clarence!
	[*Enter Warwick, Gloucester, Clarence*]
Clarence.	Doth the King call?
Warwick.	What would your Majesty? How fares your Grace?
King.	Why did you leave me here alone, my lords?
Clarence.	We left the Prince my brother here, my liege,
	Who undertook to sit and watch by you.
King.	The Prince of Wales! Where is he? Let me see him.
	He is not here.
Warwick.	This door is open. He is gone this way.
Gloucester.	He came not through the chamber where we stayed.
King.	Where is the crown? Who took it from my pillow?
Warwick.	When we withdrew, my liege, we left it here.
King.	The Prince hath ta'en it hence. Go, seek him out.
	Is he so hasty that he doth suppose
	My sleep my death?
	Find him, my Lord of Warwick, chide him hither.
	[*Exit Warwick*]
	This part of his conjoins with my disease
	And helps to end me. See, sons, what things you are!
	How quickly nature falls into revolt
	When gold becomes her object!
	For this the foolish overcareful fathers
	Have broke their sleep with thoughts,
	Their brains with care, their bones with industry.
	For this they have engrossed and piled up
	The cank'red heaps of strange-achieved gold;

For this they have been thoughtful to invest
Their sons with arts and martial exercises.
When, like the bee, culling from every flower
The virtuous sweets, our thighs packed with wax,
Our mouths with honey, we bring it to the hive,
And, like the bees, are murdered for our pains.
This bitter taste yields his engrossments
To the ending father.
    [Enter Warwick]
Now, where is he that will not stay so long
Till his friend sickness hath determined me?

Warwick. My lord, I found the Prince in the next room,
Washing with kindly tears his gentle cheeks,
With such a deep demeanor in great sorrow
That tyranny, which never quaffed but blood,
Would, by beholding him, have washed his knife
With gentle eye-drops. He is coming hither.

King. But wherefore did he take away the crown?
    [Enter Prince Harry]
Lo, where he comes. Come hither to me, Harry.
Depart the chamber, leave us here alone.
    [Exeunt Warwick and the others]

Prince. I never thought to hear you speak again.

King. Thy wish was father, Harry, to that thought.
I stay too long by thee, I weary thee.
Dost thou so hunger for mine empty chair
That thou wilt needs invest thee with my honors
Before thy hour be ripe? O foolish youth!
Thou seek'st the greatness that will overwhelm thee.
Stay but a little, for my cloud of dignity
Is held from falling with so weak a wind
That it will quickly drop. My day is dim.
Thou hast stol'n that which after some few hours
Were thine without offense, and at my death
Thou hast sealed up my expectation.
Thy life did manifest thou lov'dst me not,
And thou wilt have me die assured of it.
Thou hid'st a thousand daggers in thy thoughts,
Which thou hast whetted on thy stony heart,
To stab at half an hour of my life.
What! Canst thou not forbear me half an hour?
Then get thee gone and dig my grave thyself,
And bid the merry bells ring to thine ear
That thou art crowned, not that I am dead.
Let all the tears that should bedew my hearse
Be drops of balm to sanctify thy head.
Only compound me with forgotten dust.
Give that which gave thee life unto the worms.
Pluck down my officers, break my decrees,

For now a time is come to mock at form.
Harry the Fifth is crowned. Up, vanity!
Down, royal state! All you sage counselors, hence!
And to the English court assemble now,
From every region, apes of idleness!
Now, neighbor confines, purge you of your scum.
Have you a ruffian that will swear, drink, dance,
Revel the night, rob, murder, and commit
The oldest sins the newest kind of ways?
Be happy, he will trouble you no more.
England shall double gild his treble guilt,
England shall give him office, honor, might,
For the fifth Harry from curbed license plucks
The muzzle of restraint, and the wild dog
Shall flesh his tooth on every innocent.
O my poor kingdom, sick with civil blows!
When that my care could not withhold thy riots,
What wilt thou do when riot is thy care?
O, thou wilt be a wilderness again,
Peopled with wolves, thy old inhabitants.

Prince.　O, pardon me, my liege! But for my tears,
The moist impediments unto my speech,
I had forestalled this dear and deep rebuke
Ere you with grief had spoke and I had heard
The course of it so far. There is your crown,
And He that wears the crown immortally
Long guard it yours. If I affect it more
Than as your honor and as your renown,
Let me no more from this obedience rise,
Which my most inward true and duteous spirit
Teacheth, this prostrate and exterior bending.
God witness with me, when I here came in,
And found no course of breath within your Majesty,
How cold it struck my heart. If I do feign,
O, let me in my present wildness die
And never live to show th' incredulous world
The noble change that I have purposed.
Coming to look on you, thinking you dead,
And dead almost, my liege, to think you were,
I spake unto this crown as having sense,
And thus upbraided it: "The care on thee depending
Hath fed upon the body of my father.
Therefore, thou best of gold art worst of gold.
Other, less fine in carat, is more precious,
Preserving life in medicine potable,
But thou, most fine, most honored, most renowned,
Hast eat thy bearer up." Thus, my most royal liege,
Accusing it, I put it on my head,

To try with it, as with an enemy
That had before my face murdered my father,
The quarrel of a true inheritor.
But if it did infect my blood with joy,
Or swell my thoughts to any strain of pride,
If any rebel or vain spirit of mine
Did with the least affection of a welcome
Give entertainment to the might of it,
Let God forever keep it from my head
And make me as the poorest vassal is
That doth with awe and terror kneel to it.

King. O my son,
God put it in thy mind to take it hence,
That thou mightst win the more thy father's love,
Pleading so wisely in excuse of it!
Come hither, Harry, sit thou by my bed,
And hear, I think, the very latest counsel
That ever I shall breathe. God knows, my son,
By what bypaths and indirect crooked ways
I met this crown, and I myself know well
How troublesome it sat upon my head.
To thee it shall descend with better quiet,
Better opinion, better confirmation,
For all the soil of the achievement goes
With me into the earth. It seemed in me
But as an honor snatched with boisterous hand,
And I had many living to upbraid
My gain of it by their assistances,

Which daily grew to quarrel and to bloodshed
Wounding supposed peace. All these bold fears
Thou seest with peril I have answered,
For all my reign hath been but as a scene
Acting that argument. And now my death
Changes the mood, for what in me was purchased
Falls upon thee in a more fairer sort,
So thou the garland wear'st successively.
Yet, though thou stand'st more sure that I could do,
Thou art not firm enough, since griefs are green.
And all my friends, which thou must make thy friends,
Have but their stings and teeth newly ta'en out,
By whose fell working I was first advanced
And by whose power I well might lodge a fear
To be again displaced. Which to avoid,
I cut them off, and had a purpose now
To lead out many to the Holy Land,
Lest rest and lying still might make them look
Too near unto my state. Therefore, my Harry,
Be it thy course to busy giddy minds
With foreign quarrels, that action, hence borne out,
May waste the memory of the former days.
More would I, but my lungs are wasted so
That strength of speech is utterly denied me.
How I came by the crown, O God forgive,
And grant it may with thee in true peace live!

Prince.	My gracious liege,
	You won it, wore it, kept it, gave it me.
	Then plain and right must my possession be,
	Which I with more than with a common pain
	'Gainst all the world will rightfully maintain.

[*Enter Prince John and Warwick*]

King.	Look, look, here comes my John of Lancaster.
Lancaster.	Health, peace, and happiness to my royal father!
King.	Thou bring'st me happiness and peace, son John,
	But health, alack, with youthful wings is flown
	From this bare, withered trunk. Upon thy sight
	My worldly business makes a period.
	Where is my Lord of Warwick?
Prince.	My Lord of Warwick!
King.	Doth any name particular belong
	Unto the lodging where I first did swoon?
Warwick.	'Tis called "Jerusalem," my noble lord.
King.	Laud be to God! Even there my life must end.
	It hath been prophesied to me many years
	I should not die but "in Jerusalem,"
	Which vainly I supposed the Holy Land.
	But bear me to that chamber; there I'll lie.
	In that "Jerusalem" shall Harry die.

[*Exeunt*]

PART II ACT FIVE

[Enter Shallow, Falstaff, and Bardolph and Page]

Shallow. By cock and pie, sir, you shall not away tonight. What, Davy, I say!

Falstaff. You must excuse me, Master Robert Shallow.

Shallow. I will not excuse you. You shall not be excused. Excuses shall not be admitted. There is no excuse shall serve. You shall not be excused. Why, Davy!

[Enter Davy]

Davy. Here, sir.

Shallow. Davy, Davy, Davy, Davy, let me see, Davy. Let me see, Davy, let me see. Yea, marry, William cook, bid him come hither. Sir John, you shall not be excused.

Davy. Marry, sir, thus, those precepts cannot be served. And, again, sir, shall we sow the headland with wheat?

Shallow. With red wheat, Davy. But for William cook — are there no young pigeons?

Davy. Yes, sir. Here is now the smith's note for shoeing and plow-irons.

Shallow. Let it be cast and paid. Sir John, you shall not be excused.

Davy. Now, sir, a new link to the bucket must needs be had. And, sir, do you mean to stop any of William's wages, about the sack he lost the other day at Hinckley Fair?

Shallow. 'A shall answer it. Some pigeons, Davy, a couple of short-legged hens, a joint of mutton, and any pretty little tiny kickshaws, tell William cook.

Davy. Doth the man of war stay all night, sir?

Shallow. Yea, Davy. I will use him well. A friend i' th' court is better than a penny in purse. Use his men well, Davy, for they are arrant knaves and will backbite.

Davy. No worse than they are backbitten, sir, for they have marvelous foul linen.

Shallow. Well conceited, Davy. About thy business, Davy.

Davy. I beseech you, sir, to countenance William Visor of Woncot against Clement Perkes o' th' hill.

Shallow. There is many complaints, Davy, against that Visor. That Visor is an arrant knave, on my knowledge.

Davy. I grant your worship that he is a knave, sir, but yet, God forbid, sir, but a knave should have some countenance at his friend's request. An honest man, sir, is able to speak for himself, when a knave is not. I have served your worship truly, sir, this eight years—and I cannot once or twice in a quarter bear out a knave against an honest man, I have but a very little credit with your worship. The knave is mine honest friend, sir. Therefore, I beseech you, let him be countenanced.

Shallow. Go to, I say he shall have no wrong. Look about, Davy! [*Exit Davy*] Where are you, Sir John? Come, come, come, off with your boots. Give me your hand, Master Bardolph.

Bardolph. I am glad to see your worship.

Shallow. I thank thee with my heart, kind Master Bardolph. [*To the Page*] And welcome, my tall fellow. Come, Sir John.

Falstaff. I'll follow you, good Master Robert Shallow. [*Exit Shallow*] Bardolph, look to our horses. [*Exeunt Bardolph and Page*] If I were sawed into quantities, I should make four dozen of such bearded hermits' staves as Master Shallow. It is a wonderful thing to see the semblable coherence of his men's spirits and his. They, by observing him, do bear themselves like foolish justices. He, by conversing with them, is turned into a justice-like servingman. Their spirits are so married in conjunction with the participation of society that they flock together in consent, like so many wild geese. If I had a suit to Master Shallow, I would humor his men with the imputation of being near their master. If to his men, I would curry with Master Shallow that no man could better command his servants. It is certain that either wise bearing or ignorant carriage is caught, as men take diseases, one of another. Therefore let men take heed of their company. I will devise matter enough out of this Shallow to keep Prince Harry in continual laughter the wearing out of six fashions, which is four terms, or two actions, and 'a shall laugh without intervallums. O, it is much that a lie with a slight oath and a jest with a sad brow will do with a fellow that never had the ache in his shoulders! O, you shall see him laugh till his face be like a wet cloak ill laid up!

Shallow. [*Within*] Sir John!

Falstaff. I come, Master Shallow. I come, Master Shallow.

[*Exit*]

*[Enter the Earl of Warwick and
the Lord Chief Justice, meeting]*

Warwick. How now, my Lord Chief Justice! Whither away?

Chief Justice. How doth the King?

Warwick. Exceeding well. His cares are now all ended.

Chief Justice. I hope, not dead.

Warwick.   He's walked the way of nature,
And to our purposes he lives no more.

Chief Justice. I would his Majesty had called me with him.
The service that I truly did his life
Hath left me open to all injuries.

Warwick. Indeed I think the young king loves you not.

Chief Justice. I know he doth not, and do arm myself
To welcome the condition of the time,
Which cannot look more hideously upon me
Than I have drawn it in my fantasy.

*[Enter Prince John of Lancaster, with Thomas
of Clarence, and Humphrey of Gloucester]*

Warwick. Here come the heavy issue of dead Harry.
O that the living Harry had the temper
Of he, the worst of these three gentlemen!
How many nobles then should hold their places
That must strike sail to spirits of vile sort!

Chief Justice. O God, I fear all will be overturned!

Lancaster. Good morrow, cousin Warwick, good morrow.

Gloucester & Clarence.	Good morrow, cousin.
Lancaster.	We meet like men that had forgot to speak.
Warwick.	We do remember, but our argument
	Is all too heavy to admit much talk.
Lancaster.	Well, peace be with him that hath made us heavy.
Chief Justice.	Peace be with us, lest we be heavier.
Gloucester.	O, good my lord, you have lost a friend indeed,
	And I dare swear you borrow not that face
	Of seeming sorrow—it is sure your own.
Lancaster.	Though no man be assured what grace to find,
	You stand in coldest expectation.
	I am the sorrier. Would 'twere otherwise.
Clarence.	Well, you must now speak Sir John Falstaff fair,
	Which swims against your stream of quality.
Chief Justice.	Sweet Princes, what I did, I did in honor,
	Led by th' impartial conduct of my soul,
	And never shall you see that I will beg
	A ragged and forestalled remission.
	If truth and upright innocency fail me,
	I'll to the King my master that is dead,
	And tell him who hath sent me after him.
Warwick.	Here comes the Prince.

> [*Enter the Prince, now King*
> *Henry the Fifth, and Blunt*]

Chief Justice.	Good morrow, and God save your Majesty!

King.	This new and gorgeous garment, majesty,
	Sits not so easy on me as you think.
	Brothers, you mix your sadness with some fear.
	This is the English, not the Turkish court.
	Not Amurath an Amurath succeeds,
	But Harry Harry. Yet be sad, good brothers,
	For, by my faith, it very well becomes you.
	Sorrow so royally in you appears
	That I will deeply put the fashion on
	And wear it in my heart. Why then, be sad,
	But entertain no more of it, good brothers,
	Than a joint burden laid upon us all.
	For me, by heaven, I bid you be assured,
	I'll be your father and your brother too.
	Let me but bear your love, I'll bear your cares.
	Yet weep that Harry's dead, and so will I,
	But Harry lives, that shall convert those tears
	By number into hours of happiness.
Brothers.	We hope no otherwise from your Majesty.
King.	You all look strangely on me. [*To the Chief Justice*] And you most.
	You are, I think, assured I love you not.
Chief Justice.	I am assured, if I be measured rightly,
	Your Majesty hath no just cause to hate me.

King. No?
How might a prince of my great hopes forget
So great indignities you laid upon me?
What! Rate, rebuke, and roughly send to prison
Th' immediate heir of England! Was this easy?
May this be washed in Lethe, and forgotten?

Chief Justice. I then did use the person of your father.
The image of his power lay then in me.
And, in th' administration of his law,
Whiles I was busy for the commonwealth,
Your Highness pleased to forget my place,
The majesty and power of law and justice,
The image of the King whom I presented,
And struck me in my very seat of judgment.
Whereon, as an offender to your father,
I gave bold way to my authority
And did commit you. If the deed were ill,
Be you contented, wearing now the garland,
To have a son set your decrees at nought?
To pluck down justice from your awful bench?
To trip the course of law and blunt the sword
That guards the peace and safety of your person?
Nay, more, to spurn at your most royal image
And mock your workings in a second body?
Question your royal thoughts. Make the case yours.
Be now the father and propose a son:
Hear your own dignity so much profaned,

See your most dreadful laws so loosely slighted,
Behold yourself so by a son disdained,
And then imagine me taking your part
And in your power soft silencing your son.
After this cold considerance, sentence me,
And, as you are a king, speak in your state
What I have done that misbecame my place,
My person, or my liege's sovereignty.

King. You are right, Justice, and you weigh this well.
Therefore still bear the balance and the sword.
And I do wish your honors may increase,
Till you do live to see a son of mine
Offend you—and obey you—as I did.
So shall I live to speak my father's words:
"Happy am I, that have a man so bold
That dares do justice on my proper son,
And not less happy, having such a son
That would deliver up his greatness so
Into the hands of justice." You did commit me.
For, which, I do commit into your hand
Th' unstained sword that you have used to bear,
With this remembrance, that you use the same
With the like bold, just, and impartial spirit
As you have done 'gainst me. There is my hand.
You shall be as a father to my youth.
My voice shall sound as you do prompt mine ear,
And I will stoop and humble my intents

To your well-practiced wise directions.
And, Princes all, believe me, I beseech you,
My father is gone wild into his grave,
For in his tomb lie my affections,
And with his spirits sadly I survive,
To mock the expectation of the world,
To frustrate prophecies, and to raze out
Rotten opinion, who hath writ me down
After my seeming. The tide of blood in me
Hath proudly flowed in vanity till now.
Now doth it turn and ebb back to the sea,
Where it shall mingle with the state of floods
And flow henceforth in formal majesty.
Now call we our high court of parliament.
And let us choose such limbs of noble counsel
That the great body of our state may go
In equal rank with the best-governed nation;
That war, or peace, or both at once, may be
As things acquainted and familiar to us,
In which you, father, shall have foremost hand.
Our coronation done, we will accite,
As I before rememb'red, all our state.
And, God consigning to my good intents,
No prince nor peer shall have just cause to say,
God shorten Harry's happy life one day!

    [Exeunt]

SCENE III

JUSTICE SHALLOW'S HOME

[Enter Sir John Falstaff, Shallow,
Silence, Davy, Bardolph, a Page]

Shallow. Nay, you shall see my orchard, where, in an arbor, we will eat a last year's pippin
of mine own graffing, with a dish of caraways, and so forth. Come, cousin
Silence. And then to bed.

Falstaff. 'Fore God, you have here a goodly dwelling and a rich.

Shallow. Barren, barren, barren. Beggars all, beggars all, Sir John. Marry, good air. Spread,
Davy, spread, Davy. Well said, Davy.

Falstaff. This Davy serves you for good uses. He is your servingman and your husband.

Shallow. A good varlet, a good varlet, a very good varlet, Sir John. By the mass, I have
drunk too much sack at supper. A good varlet. Now sit down, now sit down.
Come, cousin.

Silence. Ah, sirrah, quoth-a, we shall

[Sings] *Do nothing but eat, and make good cheer,*
And praise God for the merry year,
When flesh is cheap and females dear,
And lusty lads roam here and there so merrily,
And ever among so merrily.

Falstaff. There's a merry heart! Good Master Silence, I'll give you a health for that anon.

Shallow. Give Master Bardolph some wine, Davy.

Davy. Sweet sir, sit, I'll be with you anon. Most sweet sir, sit. Master page, good master
page, sit. [*Makes them sit down at another table*] Proface! What you want in meat, we'll
have in drink. But you must bear, the heart's all.

[*Exit*]

Shallow. Be merry, Master Bardolph, and, my little soldier there, be merry.

Silence.	[*Sings*] *Be merry, be merry, my wife has all,*
	For women are shrews, both short and tall.
	'Tis merry in hall when beards wag all,
	And welcome merry Shrovetide.
	Be merry, be merry.
Falstaff.	I did not think Master Silence had been a man of this mettle.
Silence.	Who, I? I have been merry twice and once ere now.
	[*Enter Davy*]
Davy.	[*To Bardolph*] There's a dish of leather-coats for you.
Shallow.	Davy!
Davy.	Your worship! [*To Bardolph*] I'll be with you straight.— A cup of wine, sir?
Silence.	[*Sings*] *A cup of wine that's brisk and fine,*
	And drink unto the leman mine,
	And a merry heart lives long-a.
Falstaff.	Well said, Master Silence.
Silence.	[*Sings*] *And we shall be merry, now comes in the sweet o' the night.*
Falstaff.	Health and long life to you, Master Silence.
Silence.	[*Sings*] *Fill the cup, and let it come,*
	I'll pledge you a mile to th' bottom.
Shallow.	Honest Bardolph, welcome. If thou want'st anything, and wilt not call, beshrew thy heart. [*To the Page*] Welcome, my little tiny thief, and welcome indeed too. I'll drink to Master Bardolph, and to all the cabileros about London.

Davy.	I hope to see London once ere I die.
Bardolph.	And I might see you there, Davy—
Shallow.	By the mass, you'll crack a quart together, ha! Will you not, Master Bardolph?
Bardolph.	Yea, sir, in a pottle-pot.
Shallow.	By God's liggens, I thank thee. The knave will stick by thee, I can assure thee that. 'A will not out, 'a.'Tis true bred.
Bardolph.	And I'll stick by him, sir. [*A knock at Door*]
Shallow.	Why, there spoke a king. Lack nothing. Be merry. Look who's at door there, ho! Who knocks?

[*Exit Davy*]

Falstaff.	[*To Silence, seeing him drinking*] Why, now you have done me right.
Silence.	[*Sings*] *Do me right,*
	And dub me knight.
	Samingo.

Is't not so?

Falstaff.	'Tis so.
Silence.	Is't so? Why then, say an old man can do somewhat.

[*Enter Davy*]

Davy.	And't please your worship, there's one Pistol come from the court with news.
Falstaff.	From the court! Let him come in.

[*Enter Pistol*]

How now, Pistol!

Pistol.	Sir John, God save you!
Falstaff.	What wind blew you hither, Pistol?

Pistol.	Not the ill wind which blows no man to good.
	Sweet knight, thou art now one of the greatest men in this realm.
Silence.	By'r lady, I think 'a be, but goodman Puff of Barson.
Pistol.	Puff!
	Puff i' thy teeth, most recreant coward base!
	Sir John, I am thy Pistol and thy friend,
	And helter-skelter have I rode to thee,
	And tidings do I bring and lucky joys
	And golden times and happy news of price.
Falstaff.	I pray thee now, deliver them like a man of this world.
Pistol.	A foutra for the world and worldlings base!
	I speak of Africa and golden joys.
Falstaff.	O base Assyrian knight, what is thy news?
	Let King Cophetua know the truth thereof.
Silence.	[*Sings*] "And Robin Hood, Scarlet, and John."
Pistol.	Shall dunghill curs confront the Helicons?
	And shall good news be baffled?
	Then, Pistol, lay thy head in Furies' lap.
Shallow.	Honest gentleman, I know not your breeding.
Pistol.	Why then, lament therefore.
Shallow.	Give me pardon, sir. If, sir, you come with news from the court, I take it there's but two ways, either to utter them, or conceal them. I am, sir, under the King, in some authority.
Pistol.	Under which king, Besonian? Speak, or die.
Shallow.	Under King Harry.
Pistol.	Harry the Fourth, or Fifth?
Shallow.	Harry the Fourth.

Pistol.	A foutra for thine office! Sir John, thy tender lambkin now is king. Harry the Fifth's the man. I speak the truth. When Pistol lies, do this, and fig me, like The bragging Spaniard.
Falstaff.	What, is the old king dead?
Pistol.	As nail in door. The things I speak are just.
Falstaff.	Away, Bardolph! Saddle my horse. Master Robert Shallow, choose what office thou wilt in the land, 'tis thine. Pistol, I will double-charge thee with dignities.
Bardolph.	O joyful day! I would not take a knighthood for my fortune.
Pistol.	What! I do bring good news.
Falstaff.	Carry Master Silence to bed. Master Shallow, my Lord Shallow—be what thou wilt, I am fortune's steward! Get on thy boots! We'll ride all night! O sweet Pistol! Away, Bardolph! [*Exit Bardolph*] Come, Pistol, utter more to me, and withal devise something to do thyself good. Boot, boot, Master Shallow. I know the young king is sick for me. Let us take any man's horses; the laws of England are at my commandment. Blessed are they that have been my friends, and woe to my Lord Chief Justice!
Pistol.	Let vultures vile seize on his lungs also! "Where is the life that late I led?" say they. Why, here it is. Welcome these pleasant days! 　　　[*Exeunt*]

*[Enter Beadle and three or four Officers
with Hostess Quickly and Doll Tearsheet]*

Hostess. No, thou arrant knave, I would to God that I might die, that I might have thee
hanged. Thou hast drawn my shoulder out of joint.

Beadle. The constables have delivered her over to me, and she shall have whipping-
cheer, I warrant her. There hath been a man or two killed about her.

Doll. Nut-hook, nut-hook, you lie. Come on, I'll tell thee what, thou damned tripe-
visaged rascal, and the child I go with do miscarry, thou wert better thou hadst
struck thy mother, thou paper-faced villain.

Hostess. O the Lord, that Sir John were come! I would make this a bloody day to some-
body. But I pray God the fruit of her womb miscarry!

Beadle. If it do, you shall have a dozen of cushions again. You have but eleven now.
Come, I charge you both go with me, for the man is dead that you and Pistol
beat amongst you.

Doll. I'll tell you what, you thin man in a censer, I will have you as soundly swinged for
this—you blue-bottle rogue, you filthy famished correctioner, if you be not
swinged, I'll forswear half-kirtles.

Beadle. Come, come, you she-knight-errant, come.

Hostess. O God, that right should thus overcome might! Well, of sufferance comes ease.

Doll. Come, you rogue, come. Bring me to a justice.

Hostess. Ay, come, you starved bloodhound.

Doll. Goodman death, goodman bones!

Hostess. Thou atomy, thou!

Doll. Come, you thin thing! Come, you rascal!

Beadle. Very well. *[Exeunt]*

[Enter Strewers of rushes]

First Strewer.   More rushes, more rushes!

Second Strewer.   The trumpets have sounded twice.

Third Strewer.   'Twill be two o'clock ere they come from the coronation. Dispatch, dispatch.

[Exeunt]

*[Trumpets sound, and the King and his Train pass over the stage.
After them enter Falstaff, Shallow, Pistol, Bardolph, and the Boy]*

Falstaff.   Stand here by me, Master Shallow. I will make the King do you grace. I will leer upon him as 'a comes by, and do but mark the countenance that he will give me.

Pistol.   God bless thy lungs, good knight.

Falstaff.   Come here, Pistol, stand behind me. *[To Shallow]* O, if I had had time to have made new liveries, I would have bestowed the thousand pound I borrowed of you. But 'tis no matter; this poor show doth better. This doth infer the zeal I had to see him.

Pistol.   It doth so.

Falstaff.   It shows my earnestness of affection —

Pistol.   It doth so.

Falstaff.   My devotion —

Pistol.   It doth, it doth, it doth.

Falstaff.   As it were, to ride day and night, and not to deliberate, not to remember, not to have patience to shift me —

Shallow.   It is best, certain.

Falstaff.   But to stand stained with travel, and sweating with desire to see him, thinking of nothing else, putting all affairs else in oblivion, as if there were nothing else to be done but to see him.

Pistol.   'Tis "*semper idem,*" for "*obsque hoc nihil est.*" 'Tis all in every part.

Shallow.	'Tis so, indeed.
Pistol.	My knight, I will inflame thy noble liver,
	And make thee rage.
	Thy Doll, and Helen of thy noble thoughts,
	Is in base durance and contagious prison,
	Haled thither by most mechanical and dirty hand.
	Rouse up revenge from ebon den with fell Alecto's snake,
	For Doll is in. Pistol speaks nought but truth.
Falstaff.	I will deliver her.
Pistol.	There roared the sea, and trumpet clangor sounds.

[*Trumpets sound. Enter the King and his Train including the Lord Chief Justice*]

Falstaff.	God save thy Grace, King Hal, my royal Hal!
Pistol.	The heavens thee guard and keep, most royal imp of fame!
Falstaff.	God save thee, my sweet boy!
King.	My Lord Chief Justice, speak to that vain man.
Chief Justice.	Have you your wits? Know you what 'tis you speak?
Falstaff.	My king! My Jove! I speak to thee, my heart!

King.   I know thee not, old man. Fall to thy prayers.
How ill white hairs becomes a fool and jester!
I have long dreamt of such a kind of man,
So surfeit-swelled, so old, and so profane,
But, being awaked, I do despise my dream.
Make less thy body hence, and more thy grace.
Leave gormandizing. Know the grave doth gape
For thee thrice wider than for other men.
Reply not to me with a fool-born jest.
Presume not that I am the thing I was,
For God doth know, so shall the world perceive,
That I have turned away my former self.
So will I those that kept me company.
When thou dost hear I am as I have been,
Approach me, and thou shalt be as thou wast,
The tutor and the feeder of my riots.
Till then, I banish thee, on pain of death,
As I have done the rest of my misleaders,
Not to come near our person by ten mile.
For competence of life I will allow you,
That lack of means enforce you not to evils.
And, as we hear you do reform yourselves,
We will, according to your strengths and qualities,
Give you advancement. Be it your charge, my lord,
To see performed the tenor of my word.
Set on.

   [Exeunt the King and his Train]

Falstaff. Master Shallow, I owe you a thousand pound.

Shallow. Yea, marry, Sir John, which I beseech you to let me have home with me.

Falstaff. That can hardly be, Master Shallow. Do not you grieve at this. I shall be sent for in private to him. Look you, he must seem thus to the world. Fear not your advancements; I will be the man yet that shall make you great.

Shallow. I cannot perceive how, unless you give me your doublet and stuff me out with straw. I beseech you, good Sir John, let me have five hundred of my thousand.

Falstaff. Sir, I will be as good as my word. This that you heard was but a color.

Shallow. A color that I fear you will die in, Sir John.

Falstaff. Fear no colors. Go with me to dinner. Come, Lieutenant Pistol. Come, Bardolph. I shall be sent for soon at night.

> [*Enter the Lord Chief Justice
> and Prince John of Lancaster*]

Chief Justice. Go, carry Sir John Falstaff to the Fleet.
Take all his company along with him.

Falstaff. My lord, my lord—

Chief Justice. I cannot now speak. I will hear you soon.
Take them away.

Pistol. *"Si fortuna me tormenta, spero contenta."*

> [*Exeunt all but Prince John and the Chief Justice*]

Lancaster. I like this fair proceeding of the King's.
He hath intent his wonted followers
Shall all be very well provided for,
But all are banished till their conversations
Appear more wise and modest to the world.

Chief Justice. And so they are.

Lancaster.	The King hath called his parliament, my lord.
Chief Justice.	He hath.
Lancaster.	I will lay odds that, ere this year expire,
	We bear our civil swords and native fire
	As far as France. I heard a bird so sing,
	Whose music, to my thinking, pleased the King.
	Come, will you hence? [*Exeunt*]

FINIS—PART TWO

EPILOGUE

[Spoken by a Dancer]

First my fear, then my curtsy, last my speech. My fear is your displeasure; my curtsy my duty; and my speech to beg your pardons. If you look for a good speech now, you undo me, for what I have to say is of mine own making, and what indeed I should say will, I doubt, prove mine own marring. But to the purpose, and so to the venture. Be it known to you, as it is very well, I was lately here in the end of a displeasing play, to pray your patience for it and to promise you a better. I meant indeed to pay you with this, which, if like an ill venture it come unluckily home, I break, and you, my gentle creditors, lose. Here I promised you I would be and here I commit my body to your mercies. Bate me some and I will pay you some and, as most debtors do, promise you infinitely, and so I kneel down before you, but, indeed, to pray for the Queen. If my tongue cannot entreat you to acquit me, will you command me to use my legs? And yet that were but light payment, to dance out of your debt. But a good conscience will make any possible satisfaction, and so would I. All the gentlewomen here have forgiven me. If the gentlemen will not, then the gentlemen do not agree with the gentlewomen, which was never seen in such an assembly. One word more, I beseech you. If you be not too much cloyed with fat meat, our humble author will continue the story, with Sir John in it, and make you merry with fair Katharine of France. Where, for anything I know, Falstaff shall die of a sweat, unless already 'a be killed with your hard opinions, for Oldcastle died martyr, and this is not the man. My tongue is weary. When my legs are too, I will bid you good night.

[End with a dance]

COLOPHON

Designed by the Typographic Design Department of
Graphic Arts Typographers, Inc.
The text was set photographically, using an electronic keyboard, and
programmed onto magnetic tape in Goudy Old Style: 14-point, 6-point leaded,
and then reduced at 80%. The display type has also been set in Goudy Old Style.
Complete page negatives, ready for plate-making, were then prepared.
Printed by Georgian Lithographers, Inc., on a Miller 4-color 38-inch
perfector press, using 3M type "S" presensitized plates.
The paper, manufactured by Finch, Pruyn & Company, Inc.,
is Finch Children's Book, Vellum Finish, Bright White, Basis 70.
Binding by Sendor Bindery, Inc. Three-piece Holliston cloth, Dull Black
Levant 7X back, and Kingston Natural 35308 sides over Davey Red Label
binders board. Endpapers are Elephant Hide No. 21, Black.
Book inserted into slip case covered with Kingston Natural 35308.
Illustrations are by Jack Wolfgang Beck.

WILLIAM SHAKESPEARE:
THE FIRST AND SECOND PARTS OF
KING HENRY IV